Modern Italian Lace Crochet

Karen Whooley

OCCHI BLU
PRESS

ISBN: 978-1-7344012-0-2
eBook ISBN: 978-1-7344012-1-9

Technical Editor, Charts & Schematics: Amy Curtin
Copy Editor: Tyler Whooley
Family and Personal Photos: Karen Whooley
Sample Photography: Gale Zucker
Photo Assistant: Yliana Tibitoski
Model and Makeup: Yasmin Hasan
Book Design: Elizabeth Green

To my Nonna, Meri Parducci.

Thank you for sharing with me your love of crochet. You told me that you had given me a new skill and that you wanted me to do something with it. I hope I am living up to your expectations.

Mi manchi così tanto ma sei nel mio cuore.
Prega per me.

Advance Praise

for Modern Italian Lace Crochet

Karen's Italian heritage shines through in her beautiful collection of lace designs. This is a love letter to all our grandmothers who have passed the love of craft to the next generation. Nonna would be so proud!

—Terry Kimbrough, Crochet Designer

LEISUREARTS.COM/CATALOGSEARCH/RESULT/?Q=TERRY+KIMBROUGH

Modern Italian Lace Crochet is a true labor of love inspired by Karen's Italian grandmother. Karen has collected stitch patterns from old family resources and Italian stitch dictionaries and turned them into modern projects. Fine yarn, openwork patterning, and simple garment shapes make the designs accessible to beyond-beginner crocheters. Each project includes both full text and stitches charts, so you can follow the patterns in whatever way works best for you.

—Edie Eckman, Author of *The Crochet Answer Book* and *Around the Corner Crochet Borders*

EDIEECKMAN.COM

A classic with a personal touch, *Modern Italian Lace Crochet* has a great variety of patterns to choose from. With clear instructions and detailed charts for every pattern, you'll cherish this ode to Karen's Nonna.

—Karen McKenna, Crochet Designer
IHOOKDESIGN.COM

Weaving together the inspiration from the past with sensibilities of today, Karen Whooley reminds us of the best of our past by sharing her memories with us. As stitchers crochet pieces from this collection, they will be crafting their own treasured stories.

—Ellen Gormley, Crochet Designer, Author, and Teacher
ELLENGORMLEY.COM

My friend Karen's newest book, *Modern Italian Lace Crochet*, is a beautifully crafted book full of lovely accessories, including a few stylish lace sweaters, all of which would be excellent designs for a confident beginner, yet enjoyable for the seasoned crocheter. Karen gives you a glimpse into her Italian heritage and the endearing relationship she had with her Nonna, the grandmother who taught her how to crochet when she was a child.

—Bonnie Barker, Bonnie Bay Crochet
BONNIEBAY.COM

Contents

Architeturra ❧ 23

Costiera ❧ 31

Piazza ❧ 37

Strade ❧ 45

Introduction

Welcome to *Modern Italian Lace Crochet*.

In the pages of this book, there are a lot of memories. More memories than I can possibly share and many that I may have even forgotten over the last 46 years of being a crocheter. As you read in the dedication, this book is for my Nonna. But I like to think that it is not only *for* my Nonna, but it is also *from* my Nonna.

Let me tell you her story.

Meri (Paoletti) Parducci was born on January 6, 1903, in San Francisco. She was the second child of four and the only daughter of my bisnonni (great grandparents). Her parents emigrated from Italy in the 1890s and her father, Francesco, had a business manufacturing wagons in San Francisco. When the 1906 earthquake hit, Francesco lost everything and moved the family back to Italy. They settled in a small town outside of Lucca called

OPPOSITE PAGE:
NONNA AS A BABY
BELOW: HER 1928–29
PASSPORT

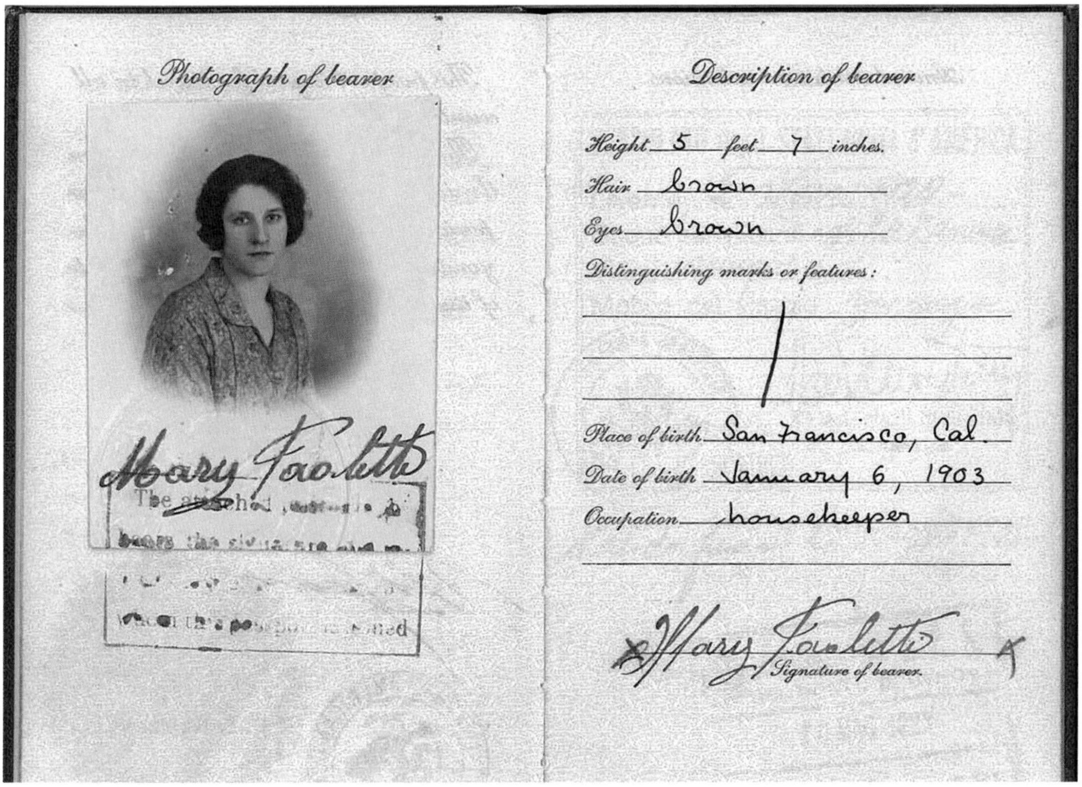

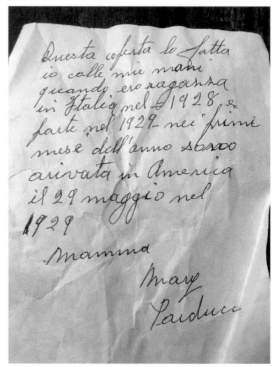

Translation of Nonna's handwritten note (above right):

I made this blanket with my hands when I was a girl in Italy in 1928 and left in 1929 in the early months of the year. I arrived in America on May 29 in 1929. —*Mamma Mary Parducci*

Guamo. Francesco opened a new wagon manufacturing business. Meanwhile, Meri learned all of the things to take care of a home, one of which is to crochet. Her mother, Dalila was very ill, so Meri's Nonna, Letizia, lived with them and was the one to teach Nonna Meri to crochet.

As most young Italian girls in the early 20th century did, Meri learned a lot of lacework. Mostly doilies and trimmings but also tablecloths and bedspreads. Meri even crocheted altar cloths for the Catholic church she attended. Then in late 1928, she boarded a ship leaving from Genoa, Italy, for the United States. She was meeting her older brother, whom she stayed with, and my Nonno in San Francisco, arriving in May 1929. In September 1929, she married my Nonno. How they met and married is another story unto itself and you can read it on my blog (karenwhooley. com/115-years)

The reason I tell that story is that I am the proud and grateful recipient of the beautiful bedspread that my Nonna crocheted in Size 10 thread. She started it in 1928 before she left Italy and finished it before her boat arrived in San Francisco. I have with it a note in her handwriting that she wrote to her daughters explaining how and when it was made. It is

my treasure. While I currently don't have a place to display it, I do pull it out from time to time to remind me about what I learned and where it all came from.

You see, when I was a little girl back in 1974 – I was seven years old – my Nonna thought I watched way too much television. One summer afternoon, when my mom brought my five-year-old sister and me over to Nonna and Nonno's house while she went to a doctor's appointment. Nonna sent Diane out with my Nonno to play in the yard and proceeded to give me a red plastic US Size G/6 (4.0 mm) crochet hook and some of that old 1970s acrylic yarn in typical colors of the era – deep green, gold, and rusty brown – where she proceeded to teach me to crochet the basic stitches.

Over the course of the next couple of hours (and yes, I was *hooked* from the first and had the attention span of a saint!) not only did I learn to chain, single, double and triple crochet, I also completed my first project. I covered a coat hanger with double crochet stitches. I even learned to weave in ends and seam with a whip stitch. I still have that hanger *and* the hook she gave me!

I still remember laying – yes, laying on my back with the armrest as my pillow – on her green vinyl couch in the basement with hook and yarn in my hand with Nonna sitting next to me helping me with those first stitches. It is one of those memories that is etched in my mind as clear as if it were yesterday.

What I learned that day, and in the months and years to follow, was a craft. Or as Nonna called it, a skill. The next time I saw Nonna, which couldn't have been more than a week, she gave me a Size 6 (1.5 mm) steel hook and Size 10 cotton and I learned to crochet lace. I don't know what happened to some of those first pieces I made, but I know Nonna took teaching me seriously.

Nonna spoke very little English, and most of that broken, so I learned to crochet in Italian. She couldn't read an English pattern, so when I went to the store with mom to get a pattern to make items for the family, Nonna and I would take a magnifying glass to the photo and figure it out by what we now call reverse-engineering. Uncinetto (crochet), punto doppio (double crochet) as well as many other Italian terms are still in my memory.

For many years I avoided the tiny yarns and hooks. But as I grew older I would pull out the bedspread and remember where my roots really are. Now I design almost exclusive-

ABOVE AND OPPOSITE PAGE:
THE AUTHOR WITH HER NONNA AND NONNO IN 1990.

ly in laceweight and fingering weight yarns. And working with those yarns brings back many memories of Nonna.

We lost Nonna in 1992. I sold my first published design in 1998. There is a huge hole in my heart because she has not been here to see what I have done with the "skill she gave me." My mom always said that she expected me to make items for charity (which I do) and for our family (which I also do) and not create a business and livelihood with it. But being the woman she was, I know she would be my first and biggest cheerleader.

I wish I could share with her the gorgeous yarns - the wools, alpacas, and silks we now have and how crochet has become an art that has developed into much more than it was in the 20th century. I do, however, think that she is up in Heaven looking down on me, smiling. She knows what I have done with crochet, and how I have taken to heart everything she taught me. And now I get to share it with all of you.

This book is a labor of love. Many of the stitches I used come from stitch dictionaries and sample pieces I have from her that came from Italy when she returned to the United States. Others are stitches from Italian stitch dictionaries I have found over the years. But all of them are rooted in what I learned from Nonna as a child.

I hope you will enjoy your time with this book and each of the patterns included. And I hope that you too will feel a bit of the history my Nonna shared with me.

Before You Start

Gauge

Gauge is probably the dirty word of crochet. Most of us don't like to take the time or, as I have heard in some of my classes, waste the yarn to check our gauge. But – especially in my experience with lace crochet – gauge can be the difference between a shawl that is just right and one that will cover an African elephant.

When looking at the gauge and which hook I recommend for each pattern, remember that the hook size is just that: a recommendation. I may crochet more loosely than you. You may have to go to a hook that is 2–3 times larger to get the same gauge. That is OK! If you have to go down a hook size to get the gauge, that is fine!

And don't forget … every pattern's gauge is the BLOCKED gauge. So not only will you need to make a swatch, you will need to block it.

Substituting Heavier Yarns

I realize many of you who don't like working with the finer yarns I used in this book. That is OK! You can substitute a heavier-weight yarn, but that means gauge is going to be even more important!

A heavier yarn means your project will grow longer and wider faster than the pattern is written. But every pattern has a repeat. So what you would need to do is make a gauge swatch following the pattern for at least 3 repeats. Block it. Then measure your gauge. You will have to do some math using your gauge to figure out how many repeats you will need to make in order for your project to come out the size you want.

There are a couple of things to note about using heavier yarns than what I used. First, the project will be bulkier than the samples shown here. You will need to play with hook sizes to be able to get some good drape with heavier yarns. And secondly, the yardage requirements will be vastly different that what I included in the pattern. Most will have less yardage but only a good gauge swatch will help you know for certain.

Reading a Crochet Chart

I believe everyone learns to read patterns differently. Some people are very visual; others can get by with just the words. That is why you will find every pattern in this book includes both written instructions and symbol charts.

To read my charts, the first thing you want to look at is the key. Each symbol represents a stitch in the pattern. It's important that you know how to make all of the stitches shown in the key. If you don't, check the special stitches section of the pattern to learn how.

You will always read the crochet chart from bottom to top. Every row or round is numbered where it begins. The odd rows will be one color, the even another. Both of these will help you to keep from losing your place. If you are working in rows, you will turn the work at the end of every row. If you are working in rounds, most often you will continue to work on the right side of the fabric. But verify in the written pattern that this is the case as often there are patterns that do need to turn the work in the round.

Normally, you will only be working into a chain when you are working into the foundation chain. However, if you see one or more stitches sitting on top of one or multiple chains, that will indicate that you will work in the chain space, not in the chain(s) themselves. But use your written pattern to be sure that is the case.

If you are working solely from the chart, you may want to use a ruler, a magnetic chart keeper or even removable highlighter tape to keep track of the row you are on. If you are in the middle of the row, using a removable flag to point out the stitch you are at can also be very helpful.

When in doubt, you can always refer back to the text of the pattern. I find that this is the best way to figure out tricky parts of the pattern.

Abbreviations

beg	begin(ning)		rs	right side
blo	back loops only		sc	single crochet
ch	chain		sk	skip
dc	double crochet		sp(s)	space(s)
dtr	double treble crochet		sl st	slip stitch
hdc	half double crochet		st(s)	stitch(es)
rep	repeat		tr	triple crochet
rnd(s)	round(s)		ws	wrong side

Yarn Weights

US	UK	AUS	Hook Size
Lace	1 ply	2 ply	1.5−2.25mm
Fingering	2 ply	3 ply	1.25−3.5mm
Sport	4 ply	5 ply	3.5−4.5mm
DK	DK	8 ply	4.5−5.5mm
Worsted	Aran	10 ply	5.5−6.5mm
Bulky	Chunky	12 ply	6.5−9mm
Super Bulky	Super Chunky	14 ply	9mm +

Blocking

Blocking is your friend! Truly! The reason you want to block your project is twofold:

- ❧ All of my gauges and finished sizes are to blocked measurements.

- ❧ Blocking your fabric will open up the spaces in the project, especially the lace projects, and create beautiful draping fabric.

Every one of the projects has been firmly blocked and you will want to do the same with yours! Never blocked before? Here is how:

First, if you are working on a garment, I recommend you block all the pieces BEFORE you sew them together. This allows you to do just a light steam later on.

Start by soaking your project in cool water with a little bit of gentle detergent for at least 30 minutes. Once the fabric is thoroughly wet, place it inside a large towel, roll it up and squeeze gently to remove the excess water. You want the fabric wet but not dripping.

Once the excess water is gone, lay out your project on your blocking surface. I use blocking mats but you can use a bed, carpet, or any other such soft surface. If you have blocking wires, weave them through the edges of the project, especially the straight ones. If you don't, you can skip this step.

Using the schematic for the project as your guide, pin out the straight edges. Make sure to tug the fabric well to start opening up any lacework. I use a yardstick or tape measure (sometimes both for extra long items) to make sure everything is straight and even. Use non-rusting T-pins for the best results.

Once the edges are straight, loosely pin out the remaining parts, such as necklines and armholes on sweaters, or the curved edges of a shawl. Flexible wires (such as the ones I list in the back of the book) are great for making scallops and points sharp and crisp. This is where you will have to really tug well to open up everything. If you have an edging that is rippled or has points or even picots, you will want to place a pin in each peak to make sure they stand open the way they need to be.

Now comes the hard part. LET. IT. DRY. Let it dry completely! In some areas you may have more humidity in your air and it will take longer than others. But if you wait, you will be very happy with the results. Once the fabric is completely dry, carefully unpin.

The
Patterns

Architeturra

Architeturra reminds me of all the gorgeous architecture in the walled city of Lucca, Italy. A study of textures, this triangular shawl looks complicated, but really starts off slowly and allows you to get comfortable as you change stitches along with changing colors. It will captivate you, just like the terracotta-colored buildings for the city that inspired it.

Finished Size

63 inches (160 cm) by 29 inches (73.5 cm), blocked

Materials

800 yards (732m) fingering-weight yarn

Sample uses Polka Dot Sheep Tenderfoot (80% merino / 20% nylon; 400 yards/366m = 3.5 oz/100g) in colors (A) Pygmy Owl and (B) Pumpkin.

Crochet Hook

Size 3.00 mm or size needed for gauge. Be sure to take the time to check your gauge.

Gauge

24 dc and 12 dc rows = 4 inches (10 cm)

Special Stitches

dc3tog: Double crochet 3 together—Yarn over, insert hook in indicated ch-3 space and draw up a loop, yarn over and draw through 2 loops on hook (2 loops remain on hook); yarn over, insert hook in next stitch (this may be a dc, dc2tog or dc3tog) and draw up a loop, yarn over and draw through 2 loops on hook (3 loops remain on hook); yarn over, insert hook in next ch-3 space and draw up a loop, yarn over and draw through 2 loops on hook; yarn over and draw through all 4 loops on hook.

dc2tog: Double crochet 2 together—[Yarn over, insert hook in next stitch or space and draw up a loop, yarn over and draw through 2 loops on hook] twice, yarn over and draw through all 3 loops on hook.

Directions

Row 1: With Color A, ch 5; [dc, ch 2, dc, ch 1, dc] in 5th ch from hook. (4 dc, 2 ch-1 sps, 1 ch-2 sp)

NOTE: Ch-4 at the beginning of each row counts as a dc and ch-1 sp unless otherwise indicated.

Row 2: Ch 4, turn; dc in first dc, ch 1, [dc in next dc, ch 1] across to center ch-2 sp; [dc, ch 2, dc] in ch-2 sp, [ch 1, dc in next dc] across to last dc; [ch 1, dc, ch 1, dc] in last dc. (8 dc, 6 ch-1 sps, 1 ch-2 sp)

Rows 3-15: Rep row 2 thirteen times. At end of row 15, change to color B. (60 dc, 58 ch-1 sps, 1 ch-2 sp)

NOTE: Ch-3 at the beginning of each row counts as a dc unless otherwise indicated.

Row 16: Ch 3, turn; 2 dc in first dc, dc in each ch-1 sp and dc across to center ch-2 sp; [dc, ch 2, dc] in ch-2 sp, dc in each dc and ch-1 sp across to last dc; 3 dc in last dc. (124 dc, 1 ch-2 sp)

Row 17: Ch 3, turn; 2 dc in first dc, dc in each dc across to center ch-2 sp; [dc, ch 2, dc] in ch-2 sp, dc in each dc across to last dc; 3 dc in last dc. (130 dc, 1 ch-2 sp)

Rows 18-20: Rep row 17 three times. At end of row 20, change to color A. (148 dc, 1 ch-2 sp)

Row 21: Ch 3, turn; dc in first dc, [ch 3, sk next dc, sc in next dc, ch 3, sk next dc, dc in next dc] across to last dc before center ch-2 sp; dc in next dc, [dc, ch 2, dc] in ch-2 sp, dc in next 2 dc, [ch 3, sk next dc, sc in next dc, ch 3, sk next dc, dc in next dc] across to end; dc once more in last dc. (36 sc, 44 dc, 72 ch-3 sps, 1 ch-2 sp)

Row 22: Ch 3, turn; dc in first dc, dc2tog over next dc and first ch-3 sp, ch 3, [dc3tog beg in next ch-3 sp, ch 3] across to last ch-3 sp before center; dc2tog over next ch-3 sp and next dc, ch 3, sk next dc, dc in next dc, [dc, ch 2, dc] in center ch-2 sp, dc in next dc, ch 3, dc2tog over next dc and next ch-3 sp, ch 3, [dc3tog beg in next ch-3 sp, ch 3] across to last ch-3 sp; dc2tog over last ch-3 sp and next dc, 2 dc in last dc. (8 dc, 4 dc2tog, 34 dc3tog, 38 ch-3 sps, 1 ch-2 sp)

Row 23: Ch 3, turn; dc in first 2 dc, ch 3, dc2tog over next dc and first ch-3 sp, ch 3, [dc3tog beg in the same ch-3 sp just worked, ch 3] across to last 2 dc before center; dc2tog over same ch-3 sp just worked and next dc, dc in next dc, [dc, ch 2, dc] in center ch-2 sp, dc in next dc, dc2tog over next dc and next ch-3 sp, ch 3, [dc3tog beg in the same ch-3 sp just worked, ch 3] across to last 3 sts; dc2tog over the same ch-3 sp just worked and next dc2tog, ch 3, dc in next dc, 2 dc in last dc. (10 dc, 4 dc2tog, 36 dc3tog, 40 ch-3 sps, 1 ch-2 sp)

Row 24: Ch 3, turn; dc in first 2 dc, dc2tog over next dc and first ch-3 sp, ch 3, [dc3tog beg in the same ch-3 sp just worked, ch 3] across to last 3 sts before center; dc2tog over same ch-3 sp just worked and next dc2tog, ch 3, sk next dc, dc in next dc, [dc, ch 2, dc] in center ch-2 sp, dc in next dc, ch 3, sk next dc, dc2tog over next dc2tog and next ch-3 sp, ch 3, [dc3tog beg in same ch-3 sp just worked, ch 3] across to last 3 sts; dc2tog over same ch-3 sp just worked and next dc, dc in next dc, 2 dc in last dc. (10 dc, 4 dc2tog, 38 dc3tog, 42 ch-3 sps, 1 ch-2 sp)

Row 25: Ch 3, turn; dc in first 2 dc, ch 3, dc2tog over next dc2tog and first ch-3 sp, ch 3, [dc3tog beg in the same ch-3 sp just worked, ch 3] across to last 2 dc before center; dc2tog over same ch-3 sp just worked and next dc, dc in next dc, [dc, ch 2, dc] in center ch-2 sp, dc in next dc, dc2tog over next dc and next ch-3 sp, ch 3, [dc3tog beg in the same ch-3 sp just worked, ch 3] across to last 3 sts; dc2tog over the same ch-3 sp just worked and next dc2tog, ch 3, sk next dc, dc in next dc, 2 dc in last dc. (10 dc, 4 dc2tog, 40 dc3tog, 44 ch-3 sps, 1 ch-2 sp)

Rows 26–33: Rep rows 24 & 25 four times. At end of row 33, switch to color B. (10 dc, 4 dc2tog, 56 dc3tog, 60 ch-3 sps, 1 ch-2 sp)

Row 34: Ch 3, turn; dc in first 3 sts, 2 dc in each ch-3 sp and dc in each st across to centerch-2 sp; [dc, ch 2, dc] in ch-3 sp, dc in each st and 2 dc in each ch-2 sp across to last dc; 2 dc in last dc. (194 dc)

Row 35: Ch 3, turn; dc in first dc and each dc across to center ch-2 sp, [dc, ch 2, dc] in ch-2 sp, dc in each dc to last dc; 2 dc in last dc. (198 dc)

Row 36: Ch 3, turn; dc in first dc, [sk 2 dc, dc in next dc, ch 1, dc in first sk dc] across to last 2 dc before center ch-2 sp; dc in next 2 dc, [dc, ch 2, dc] in ch-2 sp, dc in next 2 dc, [sk 2 dc, dc in next dc, ch 1, dc in first sk dc] across to last dc; 2 dc in last dc. (64 crossed sts, 10 dc, 1 ch-2 sp)

Row 37: Ch 3, turn; dc in first dc, [dc in next 2 dc, dc in next ch-1 sp] across to last 4 dc before center ch-2 sp; dc in next 4 dc, [dc, ch 2, dc] in ch-2 sp, dc in next 4 dc, [dc in next ch-1 sp, dc in next 2 dc] across to last dc; 2 dc in last dc. (206 dc)

Rows 38–40: Rep rows 35–37 once more. (218 dc)

Row 41: Rep row 35, then change to color A. (222 dc)

Row 42: Ch 4, turn; dc in first dc, [ch 1, sk next dc, dc in next dc] across to center ch-2 sp; ch 1, [dc, ch 2, dc] in ch-2 sp, ch 1, dc in next dc, [ch 1, sk next dc, dc in next dc] across to last dc; ch 1, [dc, ch 1, dc] in last dc. (116 dc, 114 ch-1 sps, 1 ch-2 sp)

Rows 43-54: Rep row 2 twelve times. At end of Row 54, change to color B. (164 dc, 162 ch-1 sps, 1 ch-2 sp)

Row 55: Ch 3, turn; 2 dc in first dc, dc in each ch-1 sp and dc across to center ch-2 sp; [2 dc, ch 2, 2 dc] in ch-2 sp, dc in each dc and ch-1 sp across to last dc; 3 dc in last dc. (334 dc)

Note: Ch-5 at the beginning of row counts as a dc and ch-2 sp.

Row 56: Ch 5, turn; dc in next dc, ch 2, [sk 2 dc, dc in next dc, ch 2] across to last dc before center ch-2 sp; sk next dc, [dc, ch 2, dc] in ch-2 sp, ch-2, sk next dc, [dc in next dc, ch 2, sk 2 dc] across to last 2 dc; dc in next dc, ch 2, dc in last dc. (116 dc, 115 ch-2 sps)

Row 57: Ch 4 (does not count as a st), turn; tr in first dc, [ch 6, sk next dc, sc in next dc, ch 3 (counts as a dc), turn; 6 dc in next ch-6 sp, ch 3, turn; sk first dc, dc in next 6 dc, sk next dc on row 56, tr in next dc] fourteen times; ch 1, [tr, ch 2, tr] in center ch-2 sp, ch 1; tr in next dc, [ch 6, sk next dc, dc in next dc, ch 3, turn; dc in

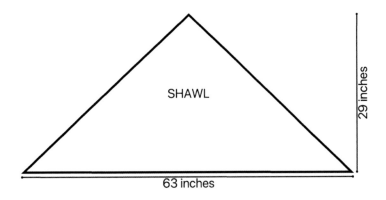

SHAWL

63 inches

29 inches

next 6 ch, ch 3, turn; sk first dc, dc in next 6 dc, sk next dc on row 56, tr in next dc] fourteen times. (28 blocks, 32 tr, 2 ch-1 sps, 1 ch-2 sp)

Note: Ch-9 at the beginning of row counts as a tr and ch-5 sp.

Row 58: Ch 9, turn; [sc in ch-3 at tip of next block, ch 5, tr in next tr, ch 5] thirteen times, sc in ch-3 at tip of next block, ch 5, tr in next tr, tr in next ch-1 sp and next tr, [tr, ch 2, tr] in center ch-2 sp, tr in next tr, tr in next ch-1 sp and next

tr, [ch 5, sc in ch-3 at tip of next block, ch 5, tr in next tr] fourteen times. (28 sc, 36 tr, 56 ch-5 sps, 1 ch-2 sp)

Row 59: Ch 3, turn; dc in first tr, [ch 2, sk 2 ch, dc in next ch, ch 2, dc in next sc, ch 2, sk 2 ch, dc in next ch, ch 2, dc in next tr] across to last 3 tr before center ch-2 sp; ch 2, sk 2 tr, dc in next tr, [dc, ch 2, dc] in next ch-2 sp, dc in next tr, ch 2, sk 2 tr, dc in next tr, [ch 2, sk 2 ch, dc in next ch, ch 2, dc in next sc, ch 2, sk 2 ch, dc in next ch, ch 2, dc in next tr] across to

end; dc once more in last dc. (120 dc, 115 ch-2 sps)

Row 60: Ch 3, turn; dc in first dc, [dc in next dc, 2 dc in next ch-2 sp] 56 times; dc in next 2 dc, [dc, ch 2, dc] in center ch-2 sp, dc in next 2 dc, [2 dc in next ch-2 sp, dc in next dc] 56 times; 2 dc in last dc. (346 dc) Fasten off. Weave in all ends.

Block to size and shape as shown in the schematic.

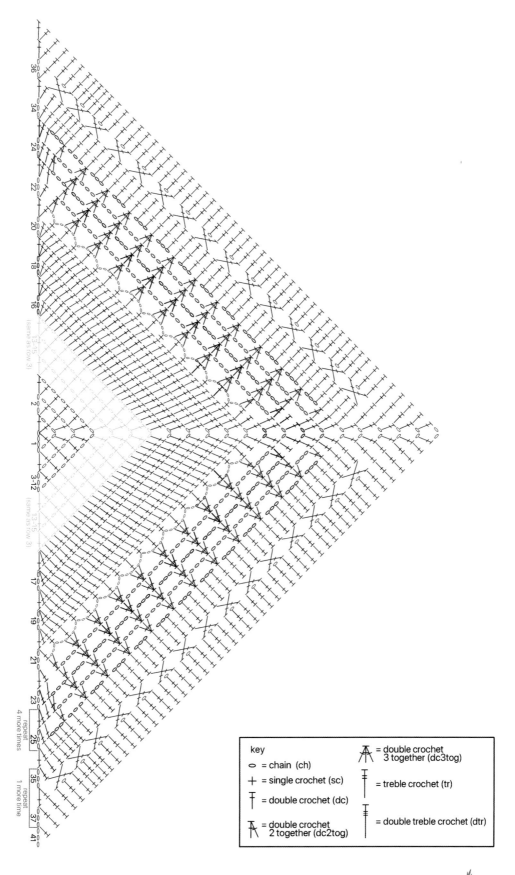

key

○ = chain (ch)

+ = single crochet (sc)

⊤ = double crochet (dc)

⋏ = double crochet
2 together (dc2tog)

⋏ = double crochet
3 together (dc3tog)

⊤ = treble crochet (tr)

⊤ = double treble crochet (dtr)

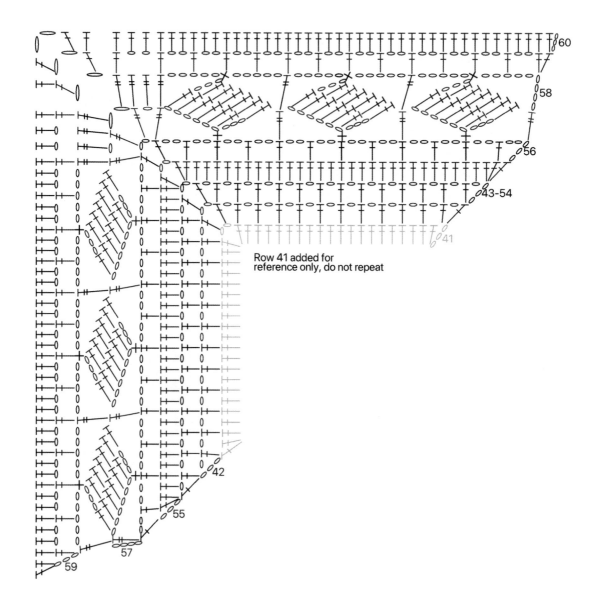

Row 41 added for
reference only, do not repeat

costiera

Summertime in Tuscany means spending time at the coast. There are many moods to the coastline from sandy beaches to rugged rocky shores. Costiera is a reminder of what ties them all together – soft, mesmerizing waves. Using a traditional Italian openwork lace, you will find you are never bored working on the subtle, undulating chevrons hidden in this gem of a shawl.

Finished Size

67 inches (170 cm) wide by 19 inches (48 cm) deep

Materials

895 yards (818 m) fingering weight yarn

Sample uses Wooly Wonka Arianrhod Sock (75% Merino / 20% silk / 5% glitter; 3.5 oz/100g = 435 yds/398 m) in the color Sea Dragon

Crochet Hook

US Size E/4 (3.5 mm) or size needed for gauge

Gauge

In dc, 20 sts and 13 rows = 4 inches/10cm

Directions

Ch 89.

Row 1: Sc in the 9th ch from hook, [ch 5, sk 2 ch, sc in next ch] twice, ch 2, sk 2 ch, dc in next 9 ch, ch 3, sk 2 ch, sc in next ch, [ch 2, sk 3 ch, 5 dc in next ch, ch 2, sk 3 ch, sc in next ch] twice, ch 3, sk 2 ch, dc in next 9 ch, ch 2, sk 2 ch, sc in next ch, [ch 5, sk 2 ch, sc in next ch] 9 times, ch 2, sk 2 ch, dc in last ch. (21 ch-sps, 29 dc, 16 sc)

Row 2: Ch 6 (counts as first st and ch-5 sp now and throughout), turn; sc in next ch-5 sp, [ch 5, sc in next ch-5 sp] 8 times, ch 5, sc in next ch-2 sp, ch 2, sk 2 dc, dc in next 7 dc, 2 dc in next ch-3 sp, ch 3, sc in next ch-2 sp, ch 5, sc in next ch-2 sp, ch 3, sc in next ch-2 sp, ch 5, sc in next ch-2 sp, ch 3, 2 dc in next ch-3 sp, dc in next 7 dc, ch 2, sk next 2 dc, sc in next ch-2 sp, [ch 5, sc in next ch-5 sp] twice, ch 5, sc in 6th ch of beg ch-8 of previous row. (20 ch-sps, 18 dc, 18 sc)

Row 3: Ch 5, turn; sc in first ch-5 sp, [ch 5, sc in next ch-5 sp] twice, ch 5, sc in next ch-2 sp, ch 2, sk 2 dc, dc in next 7 dc, 2 dc in next ch-3 sp, ch 3, sc in next ch-5 sp, ch 2, 5 dc in next ch-3 sp, ch 2, sc in next ch-5 sp, ch 3, 2 dc in next ch-3

sp, dc in next 7 dc, ch 2, sk 2 dc, sc in next ch-2 sp, [ch 5, sc in next ch-5 sp] 10 times, ch 2, dc in first ch of beg ch-6 of previous row. (21 ch-sps, 24 dc, 17 sc)

Row 4: Ch 6, turn; sc in next ch-5 sp, [ch 5, sc in next ch-5 sp] 9 times, ch 5, sc in next ch-2 sp, ch 2, sk 2 dc, dc in next 7 dc, 2 dc in next ch-3 sp, ch 3, sc in next ch-2 sp, ch 5, sc in next ch-2 sp, ch 3, 2 dc in next ch-3 sp, dc in next 7 dc, ch 2, sk next 2 dc, sc in next ch-2 sp, [ch 5, sc in next ch-5 sp] 3 times, ch 5, sc in 3rd ch of beg ch-5 of previous row. (20 ch-sps, 18 dc, 18 sc)

Row 5: Ch 5, turn; sc in first ch-5 sp, [ch 5, sc in next ch-5 sp] 3 times, ch 5, sc in next ch-2 sp, ch 2, sk 2 dc, dc in next 7 dc, 2 dc in next ch-3 sp, ch 3, sc in next ch-5 sp, ch 3, 2 dc in next ch-3 sp, dc in next 7 dc, ch 2, sk 2 dc, sc in next ch-2 sp, [ch 5, sc in next ch-5 sp] 11 times, ch 2, dc in first ch of

beg ch-6 of previous row. (21 ch-sps, 19 dc, 18 sc)

Row 6: Ch 6, turn; sc in next ch-5 sp, [ch 5, sc in next ch-5 sp] 10 times, ch 2, 2 dc in next ch-2 sp, dc in next 7 dc, ch 3, sk next 2 dc, [sc in next ch-3 sp, ch 3] twice, sk next 2 dc, dc in next 7 dc, 2 dc in next ch-2 sp, ch 2, [sc in next ch-5 sp, ch 5] 4 times, sc in 3rd ch of beg ch-5 of previous row. (20 ch-sps, 18 dc, 18 sc)

Row 7: Ch 5, turn; sc in first ch-5 sp, [ch 5, sc in next ch-5 sp] 3 times, ch 2, 2 dc in next ch-2 sp, dc in next 7 dc, ch 3, sk next 2 dc, sc in next ch-3 sp, ch 2, 5 dc in next ch-3 sp, ch 2, sc

in next ch-3 sp, ch 3, sk next 2 dc, dc in next 7 dc, 2 dc in next ch-2 sp, ch 2, sc in next ch-5 sp, [ch 5, sc in next ch-5 sp] 10 times, ch 2, dc in first ch of beg ch-6 of previous row. (21 ch-sps, 24 dc, 17 sc)

Row 8: Ch 6, turn; sc in next ch-5 sp, [ch 5, sc in next ch-5 sp] 9 times, ch 2, 2 dc in next ch-2 sp, dc in next 7 dc, ch 3, sk 2 dc, sc in next ch-3 sp, ch 3, sc in next ch-2 sp, ch 5, sc in next ch-2 sp, ch 3, sc in next ch-3 sp, ch 3, sk next 2 dc, dc in next 7 dc, 2 dc in next ch-2 sp, ch 2, [sc in next ch-5 sp, ch 5] 3 times, sc in 3rd ch of beg ch-5 of previous row. (20 ch-sps, 18 dc, 18 sc)

Row 9: Ch 5, turn; sc in first ch-5 sp, [ch 5, sc in next ch-5 sp] twice, ch 2, 2 dc in next ch-2 sp, dc in next 7 dc, ch 3, sk 2 dc, sc in next ch-3 sp, ch 2, 5 dc in next ch-3 sp, ch 2, sc in next ch-5 sp, ch 2, 5 dc in next ch-3 sp, ch 2, sc in next ch-3 sp, ch 3, sk next 2 dc, dc in next 7 dc, 2 dc in next ch-2 sp, ch 2, sc in next ch-5 sp, [ch 5, sc in next ch-5 sp] 9 times, ch 2, dc in first ch of beg ch-6 of previous row. (21 ch-sps, 29 dc, 16 sc)

Row 10: Ch 6, turn; sc in first ch-5 sp, [ch 5, sc in next ch-5 sp] 8 times, ch 2, 2 dc in next ch-2 sp, dc in next 7 dc, ch 3, sk next 2 dc, sc in next ch-3 sp, ch 3, sc in next ch-2 sp, ch 5, sc in next ch-2 sp, ch 3, sc in next ch-2 sp, ch 5, sc in next ch-2 sp, ch 3, sc in next ch-3 sp, ch 3, sk 2 dc, dc in next 7 dc, 2 dc in next ch-2 sp, ch 2, [sc in next ch-5 sp, ch 5] twice, sc in 3rd ch of beg ch-5 of previous row. (19 ch-sps, 18 dc, 18 sc)

Row 11: Ch 5, turn; sc in first ch-5 sp, ch 5, sc in next ch-5 sp, ch 2, 2 dc in next ch-2 sp, dc in next 7 dc, ch 3, sk next 2 dc, sc in next ch-3 sp, [ch 2, 5 dc in next ch-3 sp, ch 2, sc in next ch-5 sp] twice, ch 2, 5 dc in next ch-3 sp, ch 2, sc in next ch-3 sp, ch 3, sk next 2 dc, dc in next 7 dc, 2 dc in next ch-2 sp, ch 2, sc in next ch-5 sp, [ch 5, sc in next ch-5 sp] 8 times, ch 2, dc in first ch of beg ch-6 of previous row. (21 ch-sps, 34 dc, 15 sc)

Row 12: Ch 6, turn; sc in first ch-5 sp, [ch 5, sc in next ch-5 sp] 7 times, ch 5, sc in next ch-2 sp, ch 2, sk 2 dc, dc in next 7 dc, 2 dc in next ch-3 sp, ch 3, [sc in next ch-2 sp, ch 5, sc in next ch-2 sp, ch 3] 3 times, 2 dc in next ch-3 sp, dc in next 7 dc, ch 2, sk 2 dc, sc in next ch-2 sp, ch 5, sc in next ch-5 sp, ch 5, sc in 3rd ch of beg ch-5 of previous row. (20 ch-sps, 18 dc, 18 sc)

Row 13: Ch 5, turn; sc in first ch-5 sp, ch 5, sc in next ch-5 sp, ch 5, sc in next ch-2 sp, ch 2, sk next 2 dc, dc in next 7 dc, 2 dc in next ch-3 sp, ch 3, [sc in next ch-5 sp, ch 2, 5 dc in next ch-3 sp, ch 2] twice, sc in next ch-5 sp, ch 3, 2 dc in next ch-3 sp, dc in next 7 dc, ch 2, sk 2 dc, sc in next ch-2 sp, [ch 5, sc in next ch-5 sp] 9 times, ch 2, dc in the first ch of beg ch-6 of previous row. (21 ch-sps, 29 dc, 16 sc)

Rep rows 2–13 sixteen times more.

Rep rows 2–9 once more.

Last row: Ch 5, turn; sc in first ch-5 sp, [ch 3, sc in next ch-5 sp] 8 times, ch 3, sc in next ch-2 sp, sl st in next 9 dc, sc in next ch-3 sp, [ch 3, sc in next ch-2 sp, ch 2, sk 2 dc, sl st in next dc, ch 2, sk 2 dc, sc in next ch-2 sp] twice, ch 3, sc in next ch-3 sp, sl st in next 9 dc, sc in next ch-2 sp, [ch 3, sc in next ch-5 sp] twice, ch 3, sc in 3rd ch of beg ch-5 of previous row. Fasten off. (20 ch-sps)

Finishing

Weave in all ends. Block to size and shape as shown in schematic.

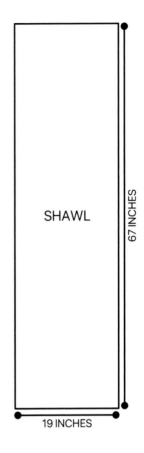

SHAWL

67 INCHES

19 INCHES

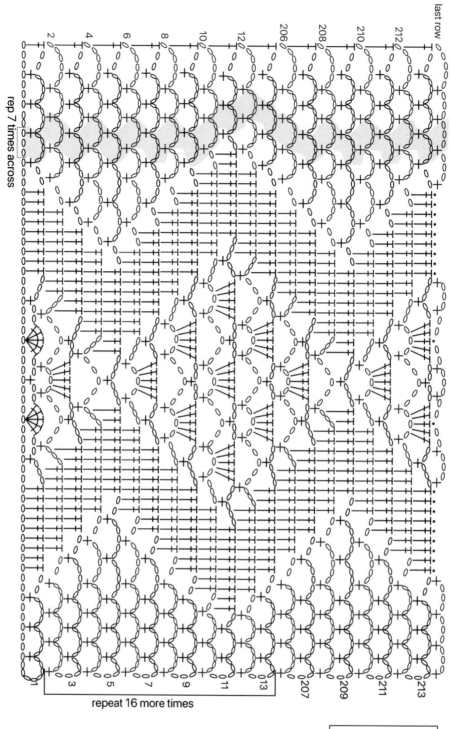

rep 7 times across

repeat 16 more times

key
• = slip stitch (sl st)
0 = chain (ch)
+ = single crochet (sc)
⊤ = double crochet (dc)
⬭ = repeat

Piazza

In Italy, the "piazze" (or "squares") are the hubs of religious, civic and political life in the city. The motif used here in Piazza is a Venetian style of crochet, which uses chains covered with single crochet stitches which is a staple of Venetian Lace. It looks oh-so complex, but only you will know how easy it is to put together this join as you go shawlette. Shhhh ... it's our secret!

Finished Size

52.5 inches (133.5 cm) wide by 22.5 inches (57 cm) deep

Materials

650 yards (595 m) fingering weight yarn

Sample uses Wooly Wonka Fibers Nimue Sock (50% silk / 50% superwash merino; 3.5 oz / 100g = 435 yds / 398 m) in the colorway Hydrangea

Crochet Hook

US Size E/4 (3.5mm) crochet hook or size needed for gauge.

Gauge

Each complete motif is 7.5 inches square

Directions

First Motif

Ch 7, join with sl st to form a ring.

Rnd 1: Ch 4 (counts as first tr); 23 tr in ring; join with sl st in 4th ch of beg ch-4. (24 tr)

NOTE: Do not turn at the end of each rnd, keep RS facing.

Rnd 2: Ch 11, sl st in 6th ch from hook (first 5 chs count as first dtr); *ch 7, sk 2 tr, dtr in next tr, ch 6, sl st in 6th ch from hook; rep from * around, ch 7; join with sl st in 5th ch of beg ch-11. (8 dtr)

Rnd 3: Sl st into first ch-6 loop, ch 5 (counts as first dtr); (2 tr, 2 dc, ch 6, sl st in 6th ch from hook, 2 dc, 2 tr, dtr) in same loop, (2 dtr, 3 tr, 2 dtr, ch 6, sl st in 6th ch from hook, 2 dtr, 3 tr, 2 dtr) in next ch-6 loop; *(dtr, 2 tr, 2 dc, ch 6, sl st in 6th ch from hook, 2 dc, 2 tr, dtr) in next ch-6 loop, (2 dtr, 3 tr, 2 dtr, ch 6, sl st in 6th ch from hook, 2 dtr, 3 tr, 2 dtr) in next ch-6 loop; rep from * around; join with sl st in 5th ch of beg ch-5. (8 fans)

Rnd 4: Sl st in each of next 4 sts and in first ch-6 loop; [ch 9, (tr, ch 4) 3 times, dtr] in same ch-6 loop, [dtr, ch 4, (tr, ch 4) five times, dtr] in next ch-6 loop; *[dtr, ch 4, (tr, ch 4) 3 times, dtr] in next ch-6 loop, [dtr, ch 4, (tr, ch 4) five times, dtr] in next ch-6 loop; rep from * around; join with sl st in 5th ch of beg ch-9. (40 ch-4 sps)

Rnd 5: Do not ch-1; 5 sc in each ch-4 sp around; join with sl st to first sc. Fasten off. (200 sc)

Remaining Motifs

Rnds 1–4: Rep Rnds 1–4 of First Motif.

Rnd 5: Use one of the following methods to join your squares. You will need the layout diagram/schematic to determine which join you are using.

One-sided Join

Rnd 5: 5 sc in first 7 ch-sps, *(3 sc in next loop, sl st in center sc of the corresponding loop on adjacent motif, 2 sc in same loop on working motif) twice, 5 sc in each of next 2 loops on working motif; rep from * twice more***, 5 sc in each remaining loop around; join with sl st to first sc. Fasten off. (6 joins)

Offset One-sided Join

Rnd 5: 5 sc in next 7 ch-sps, *3 sc in next loop, sk to set of 4 center loops on edge motif of row above (see layout diagram/schematic), sl st in center sc of 3rd center-loop on right-hand edge motif, 2 sc in same loop on working motif, 3 sc in next loop, sl st in center sc of 4th center-loop on same edge motif, 2 sc in same loop on working motif, 5 sc in each of next 2 loops on working motif, 3 sc in next loop, sl st in center sc of 3rd loop of next corner on same edge-motif, 2 sc in same loop on working motif, 3 sc in next loop, sl st in center sc of 4th corner loop on next motif of row above, 2 sc in same loop on working motif, 5 sc in each of next 2 loops on working motif, 3 sc in next loop, sl st in center sc of first center-loop on same motif of row above, 2 sc in same loop on working motif, 3 sc in next loop, sl st in center sc of 2nd center-loop on same motif of row above, 5 sc in each remaining loop around; join with sl st to first sc. Fasten off. (6 joins)

Offset Two-sided Join

Rnd 5: Rep One-sided Join to ***, joining to the next motifs on the row above, rep Offset One-sided Join from * to end. (12 joins)

Finishing

Weave in all ends, block to size and shape as shown in schematic.

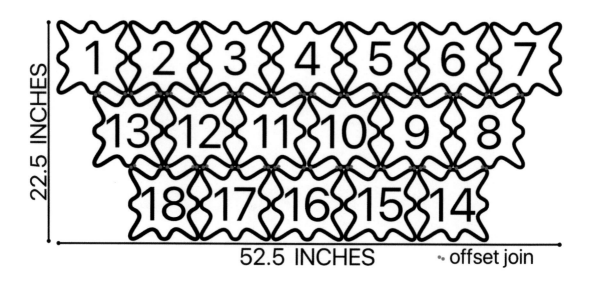

22.5 INCHES

52.5 INCHES

• offset join

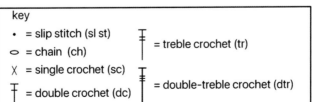

5

4

3

2

1

key

• = slip stitch (sl st)

⌒ = chain (ch)

X = single crochet (sc)

⊤ = double crochet (dc)

⊤ = treble crochet (tr)

⊤ = double-treble crochet (dtr)

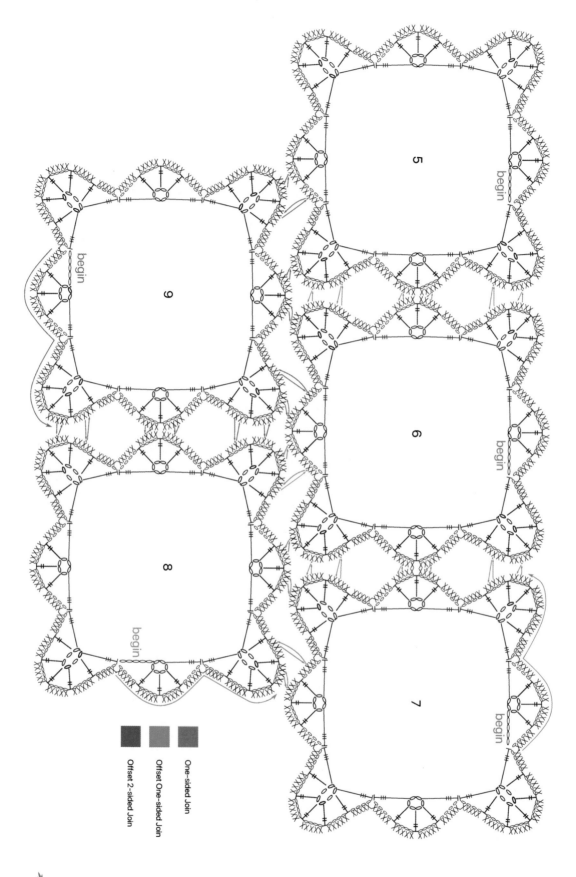

5

begin

9

begin

6

begin

8

begin

7

begin

One-sided Join

Offset One-sided Join

Offset 2-sided Join

Strade

Have you ever looked at a map of Italy? While there are some major thoroughfares, mostly you will see roads that wind and curve between each city and town, what we in America might call the "backroads." Although the lines of Strade are straight, the small floral embellishment and ladders in the texture lend themselves to the whimsy of the Italian "backroads."

Finished Sizes

S [M, L, 1X, 2X, 3X, 4X]

Finished Bust

37 [42, 48, 54, 59, 65, 70] in
94 [107, 122, 137, 150, 165, 178] cm

Finished Length

28 [28, 28, 30, 30, 30, 30] in
71 [71, 71, 76, 76, 76, 76] cm

Materials

1365 [1560, 1755, 2020, 2235, 2440, 2615] yards; (1250 [1430, 1605, 1850, 2040, 2230, 2390] m) laceweight yarn

Sample uses Anzula Breeze (65% silk / 35% linen; 4.02 oz / 114 g = 750 yards / 685m) in the colorway Birdie.

Gauge

23 sts and 11 rows = 4 in (10 cm) in pattern

Pattern Notes

The tunic is designed to have approximately 4–7 inches of ease.

Ch-3 at the beginning of each row counts as a dc.

Directions

Back

Chain 108 [124, 140, 156, 172, 188, 204].

Row 1 (RS): Dc in 4th ch from hook, dc in next 8 ch; *ch 2, sk 2 ch, dc in next 2 ch, ch 2, sk 2 ch, dc in next 10 ch; rep from * to end. (7 [8, 9, 10, 11, 12, 13] groups of 10 dc)

Row 2: Ch 3, turn; dc in next 3 dc, ch 2, sk 2 dc, dc in next 4 dc; *ch 2, 2 dc in space between next 2 dc, ch 2, dc in next 4 dc, ch 2, sk 2 dc, dc in next 4 dc; rep from * to end.

Row 3: Ch 3, turn; dc in next dc, ch 2, sk 2 dc, 2 dc in next ch-2 sp, ch 2, sk 2 dc, dc in next 2 dc; *ch 2, 2 dc in space between next 2 dc, ch 2, dc in next 2 dc, ch 2, sk 2 dc, 2 dc in next ch-2 sp, ch 2, sk 2 dc, dc in next 2 dc; rep from * to end.

Row 4: Ch 3, turn; dc in next dc, 2 dc in next ch-2 sp, ch 2, sk 2 dc, 2 dc in next ch-2 sp, dc in next 2 dc; *ch 2, 2 dc in space between next 2 dc, ch 2, dc in next 2 dc, 2 dc in next ch-2 sp, ch 2, sk 2 dc, 2 dc in next ch-2 sp, dc in next 2 dc; rep from * to end.

Row 5: Ch 3, turn; dc in next 3 dc, 2 dc in next ch-2 sp, dc in next 4 dc; *ch 2, 2 dc in space between next 2 dc, ch 2, dc in next 4 dc, 2 dc in next ch-2 sp, dc in next 4 dc; rep from * to end.

Rows 6–74 [74, 74, 78, 78, 78, 78]: Rep rows 2–5 17 [17, 17, 18, 18, 18, 18] times, then row 2 once more.

Right Back

SIZE S ONLY

Row 75: Ch 3, turn; dc in next dc, ch 2, sk 2 dc, 2 dc in next ch-2 sp, ch 2, sk 2 dc, dc in next 2 dc; ch 2, 2 dc in space between next 2 dc, ch 2, dc in next 2 dc, ch 2, sk 2 dc, 2 dc in next ch-2 sp, ch 2, sk 2 dc, dc in next 2 dc; ch 2, 2 dc in space between next 2 dc, ch 2, dc in next 2 dc. (34 sts)

Row 76: Ch 3, turn; dc in next dc; *ch 2, 2 dc in space between next 2 dc, ch 2, dc in next 2 dc, 2 dc in next ch-2 sp, ch 2, sk 2 dc, 2 dc in next ch-2 sp, dc in next 2 dc; rep from * to end.

Row 77: Ch 3, turn; dc in next 3 dc, 2 dc in next ch-2 sp, dc in next 4 dc; ch 2, 2 dc in space between next 2 dc, ch 2, dc in next 4 dc, 2 dc in next ch-2 sp, dc in next 4 dc; ch 2, 2 dc in space between next 2 dc, ch 2, dc in next 2 dc. Fasten off.

SIZE M ONLY

Row 75: Ch 3, turn; dc in next dc, ch 2, sk 2 dc, 2 dc in next ch-2 sp, ch 2, sk 2 dc, dc in next 2 dc; *ch 2, 2 dc in space between next 2 dc, ch 2, dc in next 2 dc, ch 2, sk 2 dc, 2 dc in next ch-2 sp, ch 2, sk 2 dc, dc in next 2 dc; rep from * once more. (42 sts)

Row 76: Ch 3, turn; dc in next dc, 2 dc in next ch-2 sp, ch 2, sk 2 dc, 2 dc in next ch-2 sp, dc in next 2 dc; *ch 2, 2 dc in space between next 2 dc, ch 2, dc in next 2 dc, 2 dc in next ch-2 sp, ch 2, sk 2 dc, 2 dc in next ch-2 sp, dc in next 2 dc; rep from * to end.

Row 77: Ch 3, turn; dc in next 3 dc, 2 dc in next ch-2 sp, dc in next 4 dc; *ch 2, 2 dc in space between next 2 dc, ch 2, dc in next 4 dc, 2 dc in next ch-2

sp, dc in next 4 dc; rep from * once more. Fasten off.

SIZE L [2X] ONLY

Row 75 [79]: Ch 3, turn; dc in next dc, ch 2, sk 2 dc, 2 dc in next ch-2 sp, ch 2, sk 2 dc, dc in next 2 dc; *ch 2, 2 dc in space between next 2 dc, ch 2, dc in next 2 dc, ch 2, sk 2 dc, 2 dc in next ch-2 sp, ch 2, sk 2 dc, dc in next 2 dc; rep from * once [twice] more; ch 2, 2 dc in space between next 2 dc, ch 2, dc in next dc. (49 [65] sts)

Row 76 [80]: Ch 5, turn (counts as first dc and next ch-2), 2 dc in space between next 2 dc, ch 2, dc in next 2 dc, 2 dc in next ch-2 sp, ch 2, sk 2 dc, 2 dc in next ch-2 sp, dc in next 2 dc; *ch 2, 2 dc in space between next 2 dc, ch 2, dc in next 2 dc, 2 dc in next ch-2 sp, ch 2, sk 2 dc, 2 dc in next ch-2 sp, dc in next 2 dc; rep from * to end.

Row 77 [81]: Ch 3, turn; dc in next 3 dc, 2 dc in next ch-2 sp, dc in next 4 dc; *ch 2, 2 dc in space between next 2 dc, ch 2, dc in next 4 dc, 2 dc in next ch-2 sp, dc in next 4 dc; rep from * once [twice] more; ch 2, 2 dc in space between next 2 dc, ch 2, dc in next dc. Fasten off.

SIZE 1X [3X] ONLY

Row 79 [79]: Ch 3, turn; dc in next dc, ch 2, sk 2 dc, 2 dc in next ch-2 sp, ch 2, sk 2 dc, dc in next 2 dc; *ch 2, 2 dc in space between next 2 dc, ch 2, dc in next 2 dc, ch 2, sk 2 dc,

2 dc in next ch-2 sp, ch 2, sk 2 dc, dc in next 2 dc; rep from * once [twice] more; ch 2, 2 dc in space between next 2 dc, ch 2, dc in next 2 dc, ch 2, sk 2 dc, 2 dc in next ch-2 sp, dc in next dc. (55 [71] sts)

Row 80 [80]: Ch 5 (counts as first dc and next ch-2), turn; sk 2 dc, 2 dc in next ch-2 sp, dc in next 2 dc; *ch 2, 2 dc in space between next 2 dc, ch 2, dc in next 2 dc, 2 dc in next ch-2 sp, ch 2, sk 2 dc, 2 dc in next ch-2 sp, dc in next 2 dc; rep from * to end.

Row 81 [81]: Ch 3, turn; dc in next 3 dc, 2 dc in next ch-2 sp, dc in next 4 dc; *ch 2, 2 dc in space between next 2 dc, ch 2, dc in next 4 dc, 2 dc in next ch-2 sp, dc in next 4 dc; rep from * once [twice] more; ch 2, 2 dc in space between next 2 dc, ch 2, dc in next 4 dc, 2 dc in next ch-2 sp, dc in next dc. Fasten off.

SIZE 4X ONLY

Row 79: Ch 3, turn; dc in next dc, ch 2, sk 2 dc, 2 dc in next ch-2 sp, ch 2, sk 2 dc, dc in next 2 dc; *ch 2, 2 dc in space between next 2 dc, ch 2, dc in next 2 dc, ch 2, sk 2 dc, 2 dc in next ch-2 sp, ch 2, sk 2 dc, dc in next 2 dc; rep from * 3 times more; ch 2, 2 dc in space between next 2 dc. (78 sts)

Row 80: Turn, sl st in space between last 2 dc made on previous row; ch 3, dc in same space as sl st; ch 2, dc in next 2

dc, 2 dc in next ch-2 sp, ch 2, sk 2 dc, 2 dc in next ch-2 sp, dc in next 2 dc; *ch 2, 2 dc in space between next 2 dc, ch 2, dc in next 2 dc, 2 dc in next ch-2 sp, ch 2, sk 2 dc, 2 dc in next ch-2 sp, dc in next 2 dc; rep from * to end.

Row 81: Ch 3, turn; dc in next 3 dc, 2 dc in next ch-2 sp, dc in next 4 dc; *ch 2, 2 dc in space between next 2 dc, ch 2, dc in next 4 dc, 2 dc in next ch-2 sp, dc in next 4 dc; rep from * 3 times more; ch 2, 2 dc in space between next 2 dc. Fasten off.

Left Back

With right side facing, skip 38 [38, 40, 44, 40, 44, 46] sts from the last stitch of row 75 [75, 75, 79, 79, 79, 79] and join in next stitch with a sl st.

SIZE S ONLY

Row 75: Ch 3; dc in next dc; *ch 2, 2 dc in space between next 2 dc, ch 2, dc in next 2 dc, ch 2, sk 2 dc, 2 dc in next ch-2 sp, ch 2, sk 2 dc, dc in next 2 dc; rep from * once more. (34 sts)

Row 76: Ch 3, turn; dc in next dc, 2 dc in next ch-2 sp, ch 2, sk 2 dc, 2 dc in next ch-2 sp, dc in next 2 dc; ch 2, 2 dc in space between next 2 dc, ch 2, dc in next 2 dc, 2 dc in next ch-2 sp, ch 2, sk 2 dc, 2 dc in next ch-2 sp, dc in next 2 dc; ch 2, 2 dc in space between next 2 dc, ch 2, dc in next 2 dc.

Row 77: Ch 3, turn; dc in next dc, *ch 2, 2 dc in space between next 2 dc, ch 2, dc in next 4 dc, 2 dc in next ch-2 sp, dc in next 4 dc; rep from * once more. Fasten off.

SIZE M ONLY

Row 75: Ch 3; dc in next dc, ch 2, sk 2 dc, 2 dc in next ch-2 sp, ch 2, sk 2 dc, dc in next 2 dc; *ch 2, 2 dc in space between next 2 dc, ch 2, dc in next 2 dc, ch 2, sk 2 dc, 2 dc in next ch-2 sp, ch 2, sk 2 dc, dc in next 2 dc; rep from * once more. (42 sts)

Row 76: Ch 3, turn; dc in next dc, 2 dc in next ch-2 sp, ch 2, sk 2 dc, 2 dc in next ch-2 sp, dc in next 2 dc; *ch 2, 2 dc in space between next 2 dc, ch 2, dc in next 2 dc, 2 dc in next ch-2 sp, ch 2, sk 2 dc, 2 dc in next ch-2 sp, dc in next 2 dc; rep from * once more.

Row 77: Ch 3, turn; dc in next 3 dc, 2 dc in next ch-2 sp, dc in next 4 dc; *ch 2, 2 dc in space between next 2 dc, ch 2, dc in next 4 dc, 2 dc in next ch-2 sp, dc in next 4 dc; rep from * once more. Fasten off.

SIZE L [2X] ONLY

Row 75 [79]: Ch 5 (counts as first dc and next ch-2); 2 dc in space between next 2 dc, ch 2, dc in next 2 dc, ch 2, sk 2 dc, 2 dc in next ch-2 sp, ch 2, sk 2 dc, dc in next 2 dc, *ch 2, 2 dc in space between next 2 dc, ch 2, dc in next 2 dc, ch 2, sk 2 dc, 2 dc in next ch-2 sp, ch 2, sk 2 dc,

dc in next 2 dc; rep from * to end. (49 [65] sts)

Row 76 [80]: Ch 3, turn; dc in next dc, 2 dc in next ch-2 sp, ch 2, sk 2 dc, 2 dc in next ch-2 sp, dc in next 2 dc, ch 2, 2 dc in space between next 2 dc, ch 2; *dc in next 2 dc, 2 dc in next ch-2 sp, ch 2, sk 2 dc, 2 dc in next ch-2 sp, dc in next 2 dc, ch 2, 2 dc in space between next 2 dc, ch 2; rep from * to last st, dc in last st.

Row 77 [81]: Ch 5 (counts as first dc and next ch-2), turn; 2 dc in space between next 2 dc, ch 2, dc in next 4 dc, 2 dc in next ch-2 sp, dc in next 4 dc, *ch 2, 2 dc in space between next 2 dc, ch 2, dc in next 4 dc, 2 dc in next ch-2 sp, dc in next 4 dc; rep from * to end. Fasten off.

SIZE 1X [3X] ONLY

Row 79 [79]: Ch 3, 2 dc in next ch-2 sp, ch 2, sk 2 dc, dc in next 2 dc; *ch 2, 2 dc in space between next 2 dc, ch 2, dc in next 2 dc, ch 2, sk 2 dc, 2 dc in next ch-2 sp, ch 2, sk 2 dc, dc in next 2 dc; rep from * twice [3 times] more. (55 [71] sts)

Row 80 [80]: Ch 3, turn; dc in next dc, 2 dc in next ch-2 sp, ch 2, sk 2 dc; *2 dc in next ch-2 sp, dc in next 2 dc, ch 2, 2 dc in space between next 2 dc, ch 2, dc in next 2 dc, 2 dc in next ch-2 sp, ch 2, sk 2 dc; rep from * to last st, dc in last st.

Row 81 [81]: Ch 3, turn; 2 dc in next ch-2 sp, dc in next 4 dc;

*ch 2, 2 dc in space between next 2 dc, ch 2, dc in next 4 dc, 2 dc in next ch-2 sp, dc in next 4 dc; rep from * to end. Fasten off.

SIZE 4X ONLY

Row 79: Sl st in space before next st; ch 3, dc in same space as sl st; ch 2, dc in next 2 dc, ch 2, sk 2 dc, 2 dc in next ch-2 sp, ch 2, sk 2 dc, dc in next 2 dc; *ch 2, 2 dc in space between next 2 dc, ch 2, dc in next 2 dc, ch 2, sk 2 dc, 2 dc in next ch-2 sp, ch 2, sk 2 dc, dc in next 2 dc; rep from * 3 times more. (78 sts)

Row 80: Ch 3, turn; dc in next dc, 2 dc in next ch-2 sp, ch 2, sk 2 dc, 2 dc in next ch-2 sp, dc in next 2 dc, ch 2, 2 dc in space between next 2 dc; *ch 2, dc in next 2 dc, 2 dc in next ch-2 sp, ch 2, sk 2 dc, 2 dc in next ch-2 sp, dc in next 2 dc, ch 2, 2 dc in space between next 2 dc; rep from * to end.

Row 81: Turn, sl st in space between last 2 dc made on previous row; ch 3, dc in same space as sl st; ch 2, dc in next 4 dc, 2 dc in next ch-2 sp, dc in next 4 dc, *ch 2, 2 dc in space between next 2 dc, ch 2, dc in next 4 dc, 2 dc in next ch-2 sp, dc in next 4 dc; rep from * to end. Fasten off.

Front

Chain 108 [124, 140, 156, 172, 188, 204].

Row 1 (RS): Dc in 4th ch from hook and in next 8 ch, *ch 2, sk 2 ch, dc in next 2 ch, ch 2, sk 2 ch, dc in next 10 ch; rep from * to end. (7 [8, 9, 10, 11, 12, 13] groups of 10 dc)

Row 2: Ch 3, turn; dc in next 3 dc, ch 2, sk 2 dc, dc in next 4 dc; *ch 2, 2 dc in space between next 2 dc, ch 2, dc in next 4 dc, ch 2, sk 2 dc, dc in next 4 dc; rep from * to end.

Row 3: Ch 3, turn; dc in next dc, ch 2, sk 2 dc, 2 dc in next ch-2 sp, ch 2, sk 2 dc, dc in next 2 dc; *ch 2, 2 dc in space between next 2 dc, ch 2, dc in next 2 dc, ch 2, sk 2 dc, 2 dc in next ch-2 sp, ch 2, sk 2 dc, dc in next 2 dc; rep from * to end.

Row 4: Ch 3, turn; dc in next dc, 2 dc in next ch-2 sp, ch 2, sk 2 dc, 2 dc in next ch-2 sp, dc in next 2 dc; *ch 2, 2 dc in space between next 2 dc, ch 2, dc in next 2 dc, 2 dc in next ch-2 sp, ch 2, sk 2 dc, 2 dc in next ch-2 sp, dc in next 2 dc; rep from * to end.

Row 5: Ch 3, turn; dc in next 3 dc, 2 dc in next ch-2 sp, dc in next 4 dc; *ch 2, 2 dc in space between next 2 dc, ch 2, dc in next 4 dc, 2 dc in next ch-2 sp, dc in next 4 dc; rep from * to end.

Rows 6–60 [60, 60, 64, 64, 64, 64]: Rep rows 2–5 13 [13, 13, 14, 14, 14, 14] times, then rows 2-4 once more.

Left Front

SIZE S ONLY

Row 61: Ch 3, turn; dc in next 3 dc, 2 dc in next ch-2 sp, dc in next 4 dc; ch 2, 2 dc in space between next 2 dc, ch 2, dc in next 4 dc, 2 dc in next ch-2 sp, dc in next 4 dc, ch 2, 2 dc in space between next 2 dc, ch 2, dc in next 2 dc. (34 sts)

Row 62: Ch 3, turn; dc in next dc; *ch 2, 2 dc in space between next 2 dc, ch 2, dc in next 4 dc, ch 2, sk 2 dc, dc in next 4 dc; rep from * to end.

Row 63: Ch 3, turn; dc in next dc, ch 2, sk 2 dc, 2 dc in next ch-2 sp, ch 2, sk 2 dc, dc in next 2 dc; ch 2, 2 dc in space between next 2 dc, ch 2, dc in next 2 dc, ch 2, sk 2 dc, 2 dc in next ch-2 sp, ch 2, sk 2 dc, dc in next 2 dc; ch 2, 2 dc in space between next 2 dc, ch 2, dc in next 2 dc.

Row 64: Ch 3, turn; dc in next dc; *ch 2, 2 dc in space between next 2 dc, ch 2, dc in next 2 dc, 2 dc in next ch-2 sp, ch 2, sk 2 dc, 2 dc in next ch-2 sp, dc in next 2 dc; rep from * to end.

Row 65: Ch 3, turn; dc in next 3 dc, 2 dc in next ch-2 sp, dc in next 4 dc; ch 2, 2 dc in space between next 2 dc, ch 2, dc in next 4 dc, 2 dc in next ch-2 sp, dc in next 4 dc, ch 2, 2 dc in space between next 2 dc, ch 2, dc in next 2 dc.

Rows 66–77: Rep rows 62–65 three times. Fasten off.

SIZE M ONLY

Row 61: Ch 3, turn; dc in next 3 dc, 2 dc in next ch-2 sp, dc in next 4 dc; *ch 2, 2 dc in space between next 2 dc, ch 2, dc in next 4 dc, 2 dc in next ch-2 sp, dc in next 4 dc; rep from * once more. (42 sts)

Row 62: Ch 3, turn; dc in next 3 dc, ch 2, sk 2 dc, dc in next 4 dc; *ch 2, 2 dc in space between next 2 dc, ch 2, dc in next 4 dc, ch 2, sk 2 dc, dc in next 4 dc; rep from * to end.

Row 63: Ch 3, turn; dc in next dc, ch 2, sk 2 dc, 2 dc in next ch-2 sp, ch 2, sk 2 dc, dc in next 2 dc; *ch 2, 2 dc in space between next 2 dc, ch 2, dc in next 2 dc, ch 2, sk 2 dc, 2 dc in next ch-2 sp, ch 2, sk 2 dc, dc in next 2 dc; rep from * once more.

Row 64: Ch 3, turn; dc in next dc, 2 dc in next ch-2 sp, ch 2, sk 2 dc, 2 dc in next ch-2 sp, dc in next 2 dc; *ch 2, 2 dc in space between next 2 dc, ch 2, dc in next 2 dc, 2 dc in next ch-2 sp, ch 2, sk 2 dc, 2 dc in next ch-2 sp, dc in next 2 dc; rep from * to end.

Row 65: Ch 3, turn; dc in next 3 dc, 2 dc in next ch-2 sp, dc in next 4 dc; *ch 2, 2 dc in space between next 2 dc, ch 2, dc in next 4 dc, 2 dc in next ch-2 sp, dc in next 4 dc; rep from * to end.

Rows 66–77: Rep rows 62–65 three times. Fasten off.

SIZE L [2X] ONLY

Row 61 [65]: Ch 3, turn; dc in next 3 dc, 2 dc in next ch-2 sp, dc in next 4 dc; *ch 2, 2 dc in space between next 2 dc, ch 2, dc in next 4 dc, 2 dc in next ch-2 sp, dc in next 4 dc; rep from * once [twice] more; ch 2, 2 dc in space between next 2 dc, ch 2, dc in next dc. (49 [65] sts)

Row 62 [66]: Ch 5 (counts as first dc and ch-2 sp), turn; 2 dc in space between next 2 dc, ch 2, dc in next 4 dc, ch 2, sk 2 dc, dc in next 4 dc; *ch 2, 2 dc in space between next 2 dc, ch 2, dc in next 4 dc, ch 2, sk 2 dc, dc in next 4 dc; rep from * to end.

Row 63 [67]: Ch 3, turn; dc in next dc, ch 2, sk 2 dc, 2 dc in next ch-2 sp, ch 2, sk 2 dc, dc in next 2 dc; *ch 2, 2 dc in space between next 2 dc, ch 2, dc in next 2 dc, ch 2, sk 2 dc, 2 dc in next ch-2 sp, ch 2, sk 2 dc, dc in next 2 dc; rep from * once [twice] more; ch 2, 2 dc in space between next 2 dc, ch 2, dc in next dc. (49 [65] sts)

Row 64 [68]: Ch 5 (counts as first dc and next ch-2), turn; 2 dc in space between next 2 dc, ch 2, dc in next 2 dc, 2 dc in next ch-2 sp, ch 2, sk 2 dc, 2 dc in next ch-2 sp, dc in next 2 dc; *ch 2, 2 dc in space between next 2 dc, ch 2, dc in next 2 dc, 2 dc in next ch-2 sp, ch 2, sk 2 dc, 2 dc in next ch-2 sp, dc in next 2 dc; rep from * to end.

Row 65 [69]: Ch 3, turn; dc in next 3 dc, 2 dc in next ch-2 sp, dc in next 4 dc; *ch 2, 2 dc in space between next 2 dc, ch 2, dc in next 4 dc, 2 dc in next ch-2 sp, dc in next 4 dc; rep from * once [twice] more; ch 2, 2 dc in space between next 2 dc, ch 2, dc in next dc.

Rows 66–77 [70–81]: Rep rows 62–65 three times. Fasten off.

Row 65 [65]: Ch 3, turn; dc in next 3 dc, 2 dc in next ch-2 sp, dc in next 4 dc; *ch 2, 2 dc in space between next 2 dc, ch 2, dc in next 4 dc, 2 dc in next ch-2 sp, dc in next 4 dc; rep from * once [twice] more; ch 2, 2 dc in space between next 2 dc, ch 2, dc in next 4 dc, 2 dc in next ch-2 sp, dc in next dc. (55 [71] sts)

Row 66 [66]: Ch 5 (counts as first dc and next ch-2), turn; dc in next 4 dc; *ch 2, 2 dc in space between next 2 dc, ch 2,

dc in next 4 dc, ch 2, sk 2 dc, dc in next 4 dc; rep from * to end.

Row 67 [67]: Ch 3, turn; dc in next dc, ch 2, sk 2 dc, 2 dc in next ch-2 sp, ch 2, sk 2 dc, dc in next 2 dc; *ch 2, 2 dc in space between next 2 dc, ch 2, dc in next 2 dc, ch 2, sk 2 dc, 2 dc in next ch-2 sp, ch 2, sk 2 dc, dc in next 2 dc; rep from * once [twice] more; ch 2, 2 dc in space between next 2 dc, ch 2, dc in next 2 dc, ch 2, sk 2 dc, 2 dc in next ch-2 sp, dc in next dc.

Row 68 [68]: Ch 5 (counts as first dc and next ch-2), turn; sk 2 dc, 2 dc in next ch-2 sp, dc in next 2 dc, * ch 2, 2 dc in space between next 2 dc, ch 2, dc in next 2 dc, 2 dc in next ch-2 sp, ch 2, sk 2 dc, 2 dc in next ch-2 sp, dc in next 2 dc; rep from * to end.

Row 69 [69]: Ch 3, turn; dc in next 3 dc, 2 dc in next ch-2 sp, dc in next 4 dc; *ch 2, 2 dc in space between next 2 dc, ch 2, dc in next 4 dc, 2 dc in next ch-2 sp, dc in next 4 dc; rep from * once [twice] more; ch 2, 2 dc in space between next 2 dc, ch 2, dc in next 4 dc, 2 dc in next ch-2 sp, dc in next dc.

Rows 70–81 [70–81]: Rep rows 62–65 three times. Fasten off.

Row 65: Ch 3, turn; dc in next 3 dc, 2 dc in next ch-2 sp, dc in next 4 dc; *ch 2, 2 dc in space between next 2 dc, ch 2, dc in next 4 dc, 2 dc in next ch-2

sp, dc in next 4 dc; rep from * three times more; ch 2, 2 dc in space between next 2 dc. (78 sts)

Row 66: Turn, sl st in space between last 2 dc made on previous row; ch 3, dc in same space as sl st, ch 2, dc in next 4 dc, ch 2, sk 2 dc, dc in next 4 dc; *ch 2, 2 dc in space between next 2 dc, ch 2, dc in next 4 dc, ch 2, sk 2 dc, dc in next 4 dc; rep from * to end.

Row 67: Ch 3, turn; dc in next dc, ch 2, sk 2 dc, 2 dc in next ch-2 sp, ch 2, sk 2 dc, dc in next 2 dc; *ch 2, 2 dc in space between next 2 dc, ch 2, dc in next 2 dc, ch 2, sk 2 dc, 2 dc in next ch-2 sp, ch 2, sk 2 dc, dc in next 2 dc; rep from * three times more; ch 2, 2 dc in space between next 2 dc.

Row 68: Turn, sl st in space between last 2 dc made on previous row; ch 3, dc in same space as sl st, ch 2, dc in next 2 dc, 2 dc in next ch-2 sp, ch 2, sk 2 dc, 2 dc in next ch-2 sp, dc in next 2 dc, *ch 2, 2 dc in space between next 2 dc, ch 2, dc in next 2 dc, 2 dc in next ch-2 sp, ch 2, sk 2 dc, 2 dc in next ch-2 sp, dc in next 2 dc; rep from * to end.

Row 69: Ch 3, turn; dc in next 3 dc, 2 dc in next ch-2 sp, dc in next 4 dc; *ch 2, 2 dc in space between next 2 dc, ch 2, dc in next 4 dc, 2 dc in next ch-2 sp, dc in next 4 dc; rep from * three times more; ch 2, 2 dc in space between next 2 dc.

Rows 70–81: Rep rows 62–65 three times. Fasten off.

Right Front

With right side facing, skip 38 [38, 40, 44, 40, 44, 46] sts from the last stitch of row 61 [61, 61, 64, 64, 64, 64] and join in next stitch with a sl st.

Row 61: Ch 3, turn; dc in next dc; *ch 2, 2 dc in space between next 2 dc, ch 2, dc in next 4 dc, 2 dc in next ch-2 sp, dc in next 4 dc; rep from * once more. (34 sts)

Row 62: Ch 3, turn; dc in next 3 dc, ch 2, sk 2 dc, dc in next 4 dc; ch 2, 2 dc in space between next 2 dc, ch 2, dc in next 4 dc, ch 2, sk 2 dc, dc in next 4 dc; ch 2, 2 dc in space between next 2 dc, ch 2, dc in next 2 dc.

Row 63: Ch 3, turn; dc in next dc; ch 2, 2 dc in space between next 2 dc, ch 2, dc in next 2 dc, ch 2, sk 2 dc, 2 dc in next ch-2 sp, ch 2, sk 2 dc, dc in next 2 dc; ch 2, 2 dc in space between next 2 dc, ch 2, dc in next 2 dc, ch 2, sk 2 dc, 2 dc in next ch-2 sp, ch 2, sk 2 dc, dc in next 2 dc.

Row 64: Ch 3, turn; dc in next dc, 2 dc in next ch-2 sp, ch 2, sk 2 dc, 2 dc in next ch-2 sp, dc in next 2 dc; ch 2, 2 dc in space between next 2 dc, ch 2, dc in next 2 dc, 2 dc in next ch-2 sp, ch 2, sk 2 dc, 2 dc in next ch-2 sp, dc in next 2 dc; ch 2, 2 dc in

space between next 2 dc, ch 2, dc in next 2 dc.

Row 65: Ch 3, turn; dc in next dc; *ch 2, 2 dc in space between next 2 dc, ch 2, dc in next 4 dc, 2 dc in next ch-2 sp, dc in next 4 dc; rep from * to end.

Rows 66–77: Rep rows 62–65 three times. Fasten off.

Row 61: Ch 3, turn; dc in next 3 dc, 2 dc in next ch-2 sp, dc in next 4 dc; *ch 2, 2 dc in space between next 2 dc, ch 2, dc in next 4 dc, 2 dc in next ch-2 sp, dc in next 4 dc; rep from * once more. (42 sts)

Row 62: Ch 3, turn; dc in next 3 dc, ch 2, sk 2 dc, dc in next 4 dc; *ch 2, 2 dc in space between next 2 dc, ch 2, dc in next 4 dc, ch 2, sk 2 dc, dc in next 4 dc; rep from * once more.

Row 63: Ch 3, dc in next dc, ch 2, sk 2 dc, 2 dc in next ch-2 sp, ch 2, sk 2 dc, dc in next 2 dc; *ch 2, 2 dc in space between next 2 dc, ch 2, dc in next 2 dc, ch 2, sk 2 dc, 2 dc in next ch-2 sp, ch 2, sk 2 dc, dc in next 2 dc; rep from * to end.

Row 64: Ch 3, turn, dc in next dc, 2 dc in next ch-2 sp, ch 2, sk 2 dc, 2 dc in next ch-2 sp, dc in next 2 dc; *ch 2, 2 dc in space between next 2 dc, ch 2, dc in next 2 dc, 2 dc in next ch-2 sp, ch 2, sk 2 dc, 2 dc in next ch-2 sp, dc in next 2 dc; rep from * to end.

Row 65: Ch 3, turn; dc in next 3 dc, 2 dc in next ch-2 sp, dc in next 4 dc; *ch 2, 2 dc in space between next 2 dc, ch 2, dc in next 4 dc, 2 dc in next ch-2 sp, dc in next 4 dc; rep from * to end.

Rows 66–77: Rep rows 62–65 three times. Fasten off.

Row 61 [65]: Ch 5 (counts as first dc and next ch-2), turn; 2 dc in space between next 2 dc, ch 2, dc in next 4 dc, 2 dc in next ch-2 sp, dc in next 4 dc; *ch 2, 2 dc in space between next 2 dc, ch 2, dc in next 4 dc, 2 dc in next ch-2 sp, dc in next 4 dc; rep from * to end. (49 [65] sts)

Row 62 [66]: Ch 3, turn; dc in next 3 dc, ch 2, sk 2 dc, dc in next 4 dc, ch 2, 2 dc in space between next 2 dc, ch 2; *dc in next 4 dc, ch 2, sk 2 dc, dc in next 4 dc, ch 2, 2 dc in space between next 2 dc, ch 2; rep from * once [twice] more; dc in last st.

Row 63 [67]: Ch 5 (counts as first dc and next ch-2), 2 dc in space between next 2 dc, ch 2, dc in next 2 dc, ch 2, sk 2 dc, 2 dc in next ch-2 sp, ch 2, sk 2 dc, dc in next 2 dc; *ch 2, 2 dc in space between next 2 dc, ch 2, dc in next 2 dc, ch 2, sk 2 dc, 2 dc in next ch-2 sp, ch 2, sk 2 dc, dc in next 2 dc; rep from * to end.

Row 64 [68]: Ch 3, turn; dc in next dc, 2 dc in next ch-2 sp, ch 2, sk 2 dc, 2 dc in next ch-2 sp, dc in next 2 dc, *ch 2, 2 dc in space between next 2 dc, ch 2, dc in next 2 dc, 2 dc in next ch-2 sp, ch 2, sk 2 dc, 2 dc in next ch-2 sp, dc in next 2 dc; rep from * once [twice] more; ch 2, 2 dc in space between next 2 dc, ch 2, dc in last st.

Row 65 [69]: Ch 5 (counts as first dc and next ch-2), turn; 2 dc in space between next 2 dc, ch 2, dc in next 4 dc, 2 dc in next ch-2 sp, dc in next 4 dc, *ch 2, 2 dc in space between next 2 dc, ch 2, dc in next 4 dc, 2 dc in next ch-2 sp, dc in next 4 dc; rep from * to end.

Rows 66–77 [70–81]: Rep rows 62–65 three times. Fasten off.

SIZE IX [3X] ONLY

Row 65 [65]: Ch 3, turn; 2 dc in next ch-2 sp, dc in next 4 dc, *ch 2, 2 dc in space between next 2 dc, ch 2, dc in next 4 dc, 2 dc in next ch-2 sp, dc in next 4 dc; rep from * to end. (55 [71] sts)

Row 66 [66]: Ch 3, turn; dc in next 3 dc, ch 2, sk 2 dc, *dc in next 4 dc, ch 2, 2 dc in space between next 2 dc, ch 2, dc in next 4 dc, ch 2, skip next 2 dc; rep from * twice [3 times] more; dc in last st.

Row 67 [67]: Ch 3, turn; 2 dc in next ch-2 sp, ch 2, sk 2 dc, dc in next 2 dc; *ch 2, 2 dc in space between next 2 dc, ch 2, dc in next 2 dc, ch 2, sk 2 dc, 2 dc in next ch-2 sp, ch 2, sk 2

dc, dc in next 2 dc; rep from * to end.

Row 68 [68]: Ch 3, turn; dc in next dc, 2 dc in next ch-2 sp, ch 2, sk 2 dc; *2 dc in next ch-2 sp, dc in next 2 dc, ch 2, 2 dc in space between next 2 dc, ch 2, dc in next 2 dc, 2 dc in next ch-2 sp, ch 2, sk 2 dc; rep from * twice [3 times] more; dc in last st.

Row 69 [69]: Ch 3, turn; 2 dc in next ch-2 sp, dc in next 4 dc; *ch 2, 2 dc in space between next 2 dc, ch 2, dc in next 4 dc, 2 dc in next ch-2 sp, dc in next 4 dc; rep from * to end.

Rows 70–81 [70–81]: Rep rows 62-65 three times. Fasten off.

SIZE 4X ONLY

Row 65: Sl st in space before next dc; ch 3, dc in same space as sl st; ch 2, dc in next 4 dc, 2 dc in next ch-2 sp, dc in next 4 dc; *ch 2, 2 dc in space between next 2 dc, ch 2, dc in next 4 dc, 2 dc in next ch-2 sp, dc in next 4 dc; rep from * to end. (78 sts)

Row 66: Ch 3, turn; dc in next 3 dc, ch 2, sk 2 dc, dc in next 4 dc; *ch 2, 2 dc in space between next 2 dc, ch 2, dc in next 4 dc, ch 2, sk 2 dc, dc in next 4 dc; rep from * 3 times more; ch 2, 2 dc in space between last 2 dc.

Row 67: Sl st in space before next st; ch 3, dc in same space as sl st; ch 2, dc in next 2 dc, ch

2, sk 2 dc, 2 dc in next ch-2 sp, ch 2, sk 2 dc, dc in next 2 dc; *ch 2, 2 dc in space between next 2 dc, ch 2, dc in next 2 dc, ch 2, sk 2 dc, 2 dc in next ch-2 sp, ch 2, sk 2 dc, dc in next 2 dc; rep from * to end.

Row 68: Ch 3, turn; dc in next dc, 2 dc in next ch-2 sp, ch 2, sk 2 dc, 2 dc in next ch-2 sp, dc in next 2 dc, ch 2, 2 dc in space between next 2 dc, *ch 2, dc in next 2 dc, 2 dc in next ch-2 sp, ch 2, sk 2 dc, 2 dc in next ch-2 sp, dc in next 2 dc, ch 2, 2 dc in space between next 2 dc; rep from * to end.

Row 69: Turn; sl st in space between last 2 dc made on previous row, ch 3, dc in same space as sl st; ch 2, dc in next 4 dc, 2 dc in next ch-2 sp, dc in next 4 dc; *ch 2, 2 dc in space between next 2 dc, ch 2, dc in next 4 dc, 2 dc in next ch-2 sp, dc in next 4 dc; rep from * to end.

Rows 70–81: Rep rows 62–65 three times. Fasten off.

Sleeve (make 2)

Chain 46 [46, 46, 58, 58, 58, 58].

SIZE S ONLY

Row 1: Dc in 4th ch from hook and in each ch across. (44 dc)

Row 2: Ch 3, turn; dc in next dc and in each dc across.

Row 3: Rep row 2.

Row 4: Ch 3, turn; 2 dc in next dc, dc in each dc across to last 2 dc, 2 dc in next dc, dc in last dc. (46 dc)

Rows 5–7: Rep row 2.

Row 8: Rep row 4. (48 dc)

Rows 9–10: Rep row 2.

Row 11: Rep row 4. (50 dc)

Rows 12–44: Rep rows 9–11 eleven times. (72 dc)

Rows 45–48: Rep row 2. Fasten off.

SIZES M [L, 1X] ONLY

Row 1: Dc in 4th ch from hook and in each ch across. (44 [44, 56] dc)

Row 2: Ch 3, turn; dc in next dc and in each dc across.

Row 3: Ch 3, turn; 2 dc in next dc, dc in each dc across to last 2 dc, 2 dc in next dc, dc in last dc. (46 [46, 58] dc)

Rows 4–5: Rep row 2.
Row 6: Rep row 3. (48 [48, 60] dc)

Rows 7–12 [7–9, 7–27]: Rep rows 4-6 twice [once, seven] times. (52 [50, 74] dc)

Row 13 [10, 28]: Rep row 2.

Row 14 [11, 29]: Rep row 3. (54 [52, 76] dc)

Rows 15–44 [12–47, 30–47]: Rep rows 13–14 fifteen [eighteen, nine] times. (84 [88, 94] dc)

Rows 45–48 [48–51, 48–51]: Rep row 2.

SIZES 2X [3X, 4X] ONLY

Row 1: Dc in 4th ch from hook and in each ch across. (56 [56, 56] dc)

Row 2: Ch 3, turn; 2 dc in next dc, dc in each dc across to last 2 dc, 2 dc in next dc, dc in last dc. (58 [58, 58] dc)

Row 3: Ch 3, turn; dc in next dc and in each dc across.

Row 4: Rep row 2. (60 [60, 60] dc)

Rows 5–44 [5–46, 5–40]: Rep rows 3–4 twenty [twenty one, eighteen] times. (100, 102, 96] dc)

Rows 45–47 [47–50, 41–50]: Rep row 5. (106 [110, 116] dc)

Rows 48–51 [51–54, 51–54]: Rep row 3. Fasten off.

Finishing

Weave in all ends. Block each piece to size.

Using the mattress stitch, seam front to back at shoulders.

Fold sleeves in half and line up center of fold with shoulder seam, seam sleeves to body from back to front . Beginning at hem, seam sides and continue across sleeve to cuff.

Finish neck opening: Starting at shoulder seam, evenly space sc around neckline by placing 1 sc in each stitch, 2 sc in next ch-2 sp and when working down rows, sc in side of each row and in the top of each st at the edge; join with a sl st in first sc. Fasten off.

Finish hem: Starting at one side seam, evenly space sc around the bottom by placing 1 sc in each stitch and 2 sc in each ch-2 sp; join with a sl st in first sc. Fasten off.

Finish wrist openings: Starting at seam, sc in each st around; join with a sl st in first sc. Fasten off.

Weave in all ends.

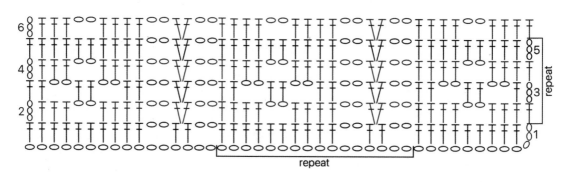

KEY

◯ = chain (ch)

† = double crochet (dc)

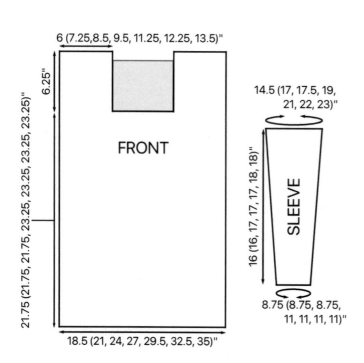

Finestrelle

TRANSLATION: WINDOWS

Finestrelle reminds me of all the open windows you will see when wandering around in a Tuscan neighborhood. Staggered squares that make the "windows" are just an easy-to-memorize six-row repeat. A quick crochet project, Finestrelle will make you want to book that trip to see those windows yourself!

Finished Size

20¾ inches (53 cm) circumference and 8½ inches (21.5 cm) tall without pom-pom. Will fit heads to 24 inches (68.5 cm)

Materials

250 yards fingering-weight yarn

Sample uses Emma's Yarn Super Silky (80% merino/20% silk; 3.5 oz/100g = 400 yards/366m) in the color Arches

Crochet Hooks

US Size E/4 (3.5 mm) and 3.00 mm crochet hooks or sizes needed for gauge

Notions

3-inch pom-pom maker tapestry needle

Gauge

With larger hook, 20 sts in patt and 12 patt rows = 4 inches

Special Stitches

Fdc: Foundation double crochet (This technique creates a foundation chain and a row of double crochet stitches in one)

Step 1: Place a slip knot on hook, ch 4 (counts as first st), yarn over, insert hook in 4th ch from hook and draw up a loop; yarn over and draw through one loop on hook (the "chain"); [yarn over and draw through 2 loops on hook] 2 times (the "double crochet").

Step 2: Yarn over, insert hook into the "chain" of the previous stitch and draw up a loop, yarn over and draw through one loop on hook (the "chain"), [yarn over and draw through 2 loops on hook] 2 times (the "double crochet"). Repeat step 2 for the length of the foundation.

FPdc: Front-post double crochet – Yarn over, insert hook from front to back and then to front again around post of stitch, yarn over and draw up loop, [yarn over and draw through 2 loops on hook] twice.

Directions

Hat Body

Rnd 1: With larger hook, Fdc 103 times; being careful not to twist, join with a sl st to top of the beg ch-4. (104 sts)

Note: Do not turn at the end of each rnd.

Rnd 2: Ch 3 (counts as first dc now and throughout); dc in next 3 dc, ch 2, sk 2 dc, dc in sp between 2nd sked dc and next dc, ch 2, sk 2 dc; *dc in next 4 dc, ch 2, sk 2 dc, dc in sp between 2nd sked dc and next dc, ch 2, sk 2 dc; rep from * around; join with a sl st to top of beg ch-3. (13 groups of 4 dc)

Rnd 3: Ch 3; dc in next 3 dc, ch 2, dc in next dc, ch 2; *dc in next 4 dc, ch 2, dc in next dc, ch 2; rep from * around; join with a sl st to top of beg ch-3.

Rnd 4: Sl st in next dc and in space before the following dc, ch 5, (counts as dc and ch-2 sp now and throughout); [2 dc in next ch-2 sp] twice, ch 2; *sk 2 dc, dc in sp between 2nd sked dc and next dc, ch 2, sk 2 dc, [2 dc in next ch-2 sp] twice, ch 2; rep from * around; join with a sl st to 3rd ch of beg ch-5.

Rnd 5: Ch 5; dc in next 4 dc, ch 2; *dc in next dc, ch 2, dc in next 4 dc, ch 2; rep from * around; join with a sl st to 3rd ch of beg ch-5.

Rnd 6: Sl st in next ch-2 sp, ch 3; dc in same ch-2 sp, ch 2; *sk 2 dc, dc in sp between 2nd sked dc and next dc, ch 2, sk 2 dc, [2 dc in next ch-2 sp]** twice, ch 2; rep from * around, ending last rep at **; join with a sl st to top of beg ch-3.

Rnd 7: Ch 3; dc in next dc, ch 2, dc in next dc, ch 2; *dc in next 4 dc, ch 2, dc in next dc, ch 2; rep from * around to last 2 dc, dc in last 2 dc; join with a sl st to top of beg ch-3.

Rnd 8: Sl st in next dc and in next ch-2 sp, ch 3; dc in same ch-2 sp, 2 dc in next ch-2 sp, ch 2, sk 2 dc, dc in sp between 2nd sked dc and next dc, ch 2; *sk 2 dc, [2 dc in next ch-2 sp] twice, ch 2, sk 2 dc, dc in sp between 2nd sked dc and next dc, ch 2; rep from * around; join with a sl st to top of beg ch-3.

Rnd 9: Ch 3; dc in next 3 dc, ch 2, dc in next dc, ch 2; *dc in next 4 dc, ch 2, dc in next dc, ch 2; rep from * around; join with a sl st to top of beg ch-3.

Rnds 10–23: Rep rnds 4–9 twice, then rnds 4–5 once more.

Rnd 24: Ch 3; 2 dc in next ch-2 sp, *dc in next 4 dc, [2 dc in next ch-2 sp] twice; rep from * to last 4 dc, dc in last 4 dc; join with a sl st to top of beg ch-3. Fasten off leaving 10-inch tail.

Bottom ribbing

Rnd 1: With smaller hook and working along the bottom of rnd 1 Fdc sts, join with a sc in bottom of beg ch, sc in remaining 103 Fdc; join with a sl st in top of first sc.

Rnd 2: Ch 3; FPdc around next Fdc 1 row below, *dc in next sc, FPdc around next Fdc one row below; rep from * around; join with a sl st in top of beg ch-3.

Rnd 3: Ch 1; sc in same st as join and in each st around; join with a sl st in top of first sc.

Rnds 4–5: Rep rnds 2 and 3 once. Fasten off.

Finishing

Using 10-inch tail at top of the hat, weave through the tops of the 104 dc around and cinch up tightly to gather the top of the hat.

Weave in all ends.

Block hat to shape.

With remaining yarn, create a 3-inch pom-pom and sew to the top of the hat.

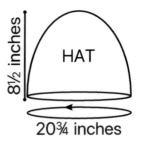

KEY

- **·** = slip stitch (sl st)
- **○** = chain (ch)
- **X** = single crochet (sc)
- = repeat
- = foundation double crochet (fdc)
- = double crochet (dc)
- = front post double crochet (FPdc)

Hat Body

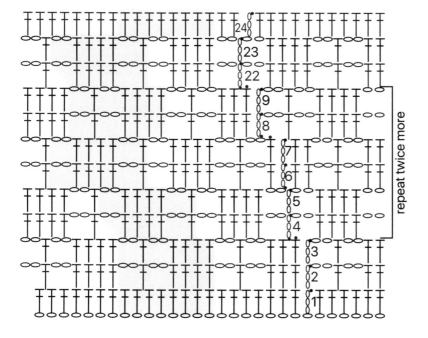

Bottom Ribbing

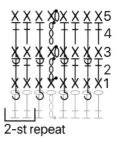

2-st repeat

Il Velo da Sposa

TRANSLATION: THE WEDDING VEIL

Soft, filmy laceweight yarn makes Il Velo da Sposa a dream to wear. Weighing next to nothing, this topper is made with two rectangles seamed at the top edge to create a poncho-style topper with clever slits to allow your arms to move freely. Beautiful, four-row repeat pattern in a traditional Italian motif makes Il Velo a classic piece for any wardrobe.

Finished Size

56 inches (142cm) wide by 16 inches (41cm) deep

Materials

1600 yards (1463m) lace-weight yarn

Sample uses Round Table Yarns Isolde (55% superwash BFL / 45% silk; 3.5 oz / 100g = 875 yards /800m) in the color Uther.

Crochet Hook

3.00 mm or size needed for gauge

Gauge

In pattern, 25 stitches and 6 rows = 4 inches (10cm)

Special Stitches

Fdc: Foundation double crochet (This technique creates a foundation chain and a row of double crochet stitches in one)

Step 1: Place a slip knot on hook, ch 4, yarn over, insert hook in 4th ch from hook and draw up a loop; yarn over and draw through one loop on hook (the "chain"); [yarn over and draw through 2 loops on hook] 2 times (the "double crochet").

Step 2: Yarn over, insert hook into the "chain" of the previous stitch and draw up a loop, yarn over and draw through one loop on hook (the "chain"), [yarn over and draw through 2 loops on hook] 2 times (the "double crochet"). Repeat step 2 for the length of the foundation.

Shell: Shell – (2 dc, ch 1, 2 dc) in stitch specified.

Pattern Notes

Ch-3 at the beginning of each row counts as a dc.

Directions

Body (make 2)

Row 1: Fdc 98 times. (99 sts)

Row 2: Ch 3, turn; (dc, ch 1, 2 dc) in first fdc; *ch 5, sk 6 fdc, dc in next fdc, ch 5, sk 6 fdc, shell in next fdc; rep from * across. (7 dc, 8 shells)

Row 3: Turn; sl st in first 2 dc and in next ch-1 sp, ch 3; (dc, ch 1, 2 dc) in same sp as last sl st; *ch 4, dc in next ch-5 sp, dc in next dc, dc in next ch-5 sp, ch 4, shell in next ch-1 sp; rep from * to end.

Row 4: Turn; sl st in first 2 dc and in next ch-1 sp, ch 3; (dc, ch 1, 2 dc) in same sp as last sl st; *ch 3, dc in next ch-4 sp, dc in next 3 dc, dc in next ch-4 sp, ch 3, shell in next ch-1 sp; rep from * to end.

Row 5: Turn; sl st in first 2 dc and in next ch-1 sp, ch 3; (dc, ch 1, 2 dc) in same sp as last sl st; *ch 2, dc in next ch-3 sp, dc in next 5 dc, dc in next ch-3 sp, ch 2, shell in next ch-1 sp; rep from * to end.

Row 6: Turn; sl st in first 2 dc and in next ch-1 sp, ch 3; (dc, ch 1, 2 dc) in same sp as last sl st; *ch 5, sk next ch-2 sp and 3 dc, dc in next dc, ch 5, shell in next ch-1 sp; rep from * to end.

Rows 7–82: Rep rows 3–6 nineteen times.

Row 83: Turn; sl st in first 2 dc and in next ch-1 sp, ch 3; *6 dc in next ch-5 sp, dc in next dc, 6 dc in next ch-5 sp, dc in next ch-1 sp; rep from * to end. Fasten off. (99 dc)

Finishing

Block each piece to 56 inches (142cm) long by 16 inches (41cm) wide.

Place one piece on top of the other with RS together; *as measured across the long edge and beginning 9" (23cm) in from right side, seam 13" (33cm) for shoulder using whipstitch; rep from * for left shoulder. See schematic for guidance.

Sections shown in light gray on schematic below are not seamed.

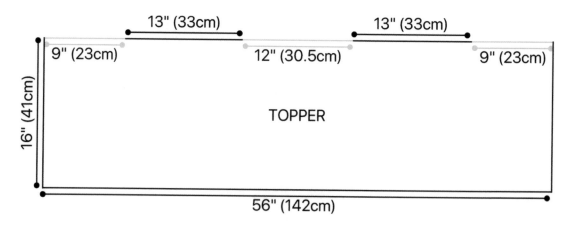

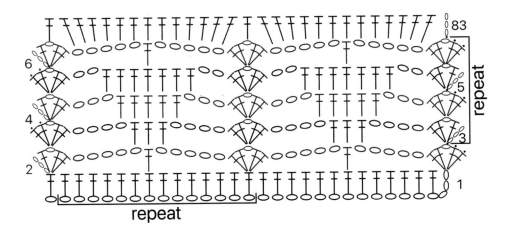

repeat

KEY

•	= slip stitch (sl st)
○	= chain (ch)
⊥	= foundation double crochet (fdc)
†	= double crochet (dc)

Maniche e Sciarpa

TRANSLATION: SLEEVES AND SCARF

Maniche e Sciarpa is a multi-purpose scarf. Leave it flat to make a wide scarf. If you use the buttons you can make an easy to wear shrug to keep your shoulders warm on a cool night. The lace in this pattern is simple to memorize and is a very traditional motif of squares and chains.

Finished Size

58 inches long by 15 inches wide

Materials

560 yards (512m) fingering-weight yarn

Sample uses Schmutzerella Yarns Spectacular (75% Superwash Merino / 20% Nylon / 5% Stellina; 3.5 oz / 100g = 438 yards / 400m) in the color 3 Up, 2 Across.

Crochet Hook

US Size E/4 (3.5mm) or size needed for gauge

Notions

Ten ½-inch (1.25cm) buttons

Gauge

in pattern, 19 sts and 8.5 rows = 4 inches (10cm)

Special Stitches

Fdc: Foundation double crochet (This technique creates a foundation chain and a row of double crochet stitches in one)

Step 1: Place a slip knot on hook, ch 4, yarn over, insert hook in 4th ch from hook and draw up a loop; yarn over and draw through one loop on hook (the "chain"); [yarn over and draw through 2 loops on hook] 2 times (the "double crochet").

Step 2: Yarn over, insert hook into the "chain" of the previous stitch and draw up a loop, yarn over and draw through one loop on hook (the "chain"), [yarn over and draw through 2 loops on hook] 2 times (the "double crochet"). Repeat step 2 for the length of the foundation.

Pattern Note

Ch-3 at the beginning of each row counts as a dc.

Directions

First Side

Row 1 (RS): Fdc 72 times. (73 sts)

Row 2: Ch 3, turn; dc in next 2 fdc, ch 7, sk 4 fdc; *dc in next 5 fdc, ch 7, sk 4 fdc; rep from * across to last 3 fdc, dc in last 3 fdc. (8 ch-7 sps, 41 dc)

Row 3: Ch 3, turn; dc in next 2 dc, ch 2, 5 dc in 4th ch of next ch-7; *ch 3, sk next dc, sc in next 3 dc, ch 3, 5 dc in 4th ch of next ch-7; rep from * across to last 3 dc, ch 2, dc in last 3 dc. (8 5-dc shells, 21 sc)

Row 4: Ch 3, turn; dc in next 2 dc, ch 2, dc in next 5 dc; *ch 7, dc in next 5 dc; rep from * across to last 3 dc, ch 2, dc in last 3 dc. (7 ch-7 sps, 46 dc)

Row 5: Ch 3, turn; dc in next 2 dc, ch 3, sk next dc, sc in next 3 dc; *ch 3, 5 dc in 4th ch of next ch-7, ch 3, sk next dc, sc in next 3 dc; rep from * across to last 3 dc, ch 3, dc in last 3 dc. (7 5-dc shells, 24 sc)

Row 6: Ch 3, turn; dc in next 2 dc, ch 7; *dc in next 5 dc, ch 7; rep from * to last 3 dc, dc in last 3 dc. (8 ch-7 sps, 41 dc)

Rows 7–61: Repeat rows 3–6 thirteen times, then rows 3–5 once more.

Row 62: Ch 3, turn; dc in next 2 dc, ch 4; *dc in next 5 dc, ch 4; rep from * to last 3 dc, dc in last 3 dc. (8 ch-4 sps, 41 dc)

Row 63: Ch 3, turn; dc in next 2 dc, 4 dc in next ch-4 sp; *dc in next 5 dc, 4 dc in next ch-4 sp; rep from * across to last 3 dc, dc in last 3 dc. Fasten off.

Second Side

Row 1: With RS facing, join with a sl st on bottom of the first fdc, dc in next 2 fdc, ch 7, sk 4 fdc; *dc in next 5 fdc, ch 7, sk 4 fdc; rep from * across to last 3 fdc, dc in last 3 fdc. (8 ch-7 sps, 41 dc)

Rows 2–62: Rep rows 3–63 of first side. Fasten off.

Finishing

Weave in all ends. Block to size.

Sew buttons in place as shown on schematic. Buttons are spaced 4¼" (11cm) apart measured center to center. The space between the stitches on the opposite edge provides the buttonholes.

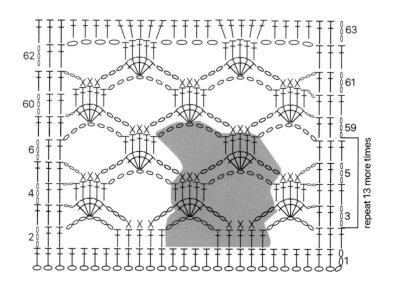

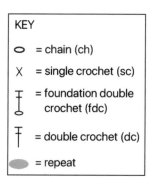

KEY

⚬	= chain (ch)
X	= single crochet (sc)
⊥	= foundation double crochet (fdc)
⊤	= double crochet (dc)
⬤	= repeat

58 inches

4.25 inches

SHRUG

15 inches

• = button

Parentesi

TRANSLATION: BRACKETS

The gorgeous lace in this wearable sweater reminds me of the gnocchi my Nonna used to make. Oblong shaped motifs are bracketed by chains that are a staple in Italian lace. Slip this top over a tank or a turtleneck for one of the most versatile pieces in your Tuscan inspired closet!

Sizes

XS [S, M, L, 1X, 2X, 3X, 4X, 5X]

Finished Bust

34.5 [38.5, 42.5, 46.5, 50.5, 54.5, 58.5, 62.5, 66.5] inches
87.5 [98, 108, 118, 128.5, 138.5, 148.5, 159, 169] cm

Finished Length

19 [21.5, 21.5, 21.5, 21.5, 21.5, 21.5, 21.5, 21.5] inches
48.5 [54.5, 54.5, 54.5, 54.5, 54.5, 54.5, 54.5, 54.5] cm

Materials

740 [870, 970, 1040, 1140, 1210, 1310, 1440, 1550] yards
(680 [800, 890, 960, 1050, 1110, 1200, 1320, 1420] m) fingering-weight yarn

Sample uses Emma's Yarn Beautifully Basic (100% Superwash Merino; 3.5 oz / 100 g = 438 yards / 400 m) in the color Wish You Were Beer.

Crochet Hook

US Size E/4 (3.5 mm) or size needed for gauge.

Notions

4 locking stitch markers

Gauge

In pattern: 24 sts and 9.75 rows = 4 inches (10 cm) blocked

Special Stitches

Fdc: Foundation double crochet (This technique creates a foundation chain and a row of double crochet stitches in one)

Step 1: Place a slip knot on hook, ch 4, yarn over, insert hook in 4th ch from hook and draw up a loop; yarn over and draw through one loop on hook (the "chain"); [yarn over and draw through 2 loops on hook] 2 times (the "double crochet").

Step 2: Yarn over, insert hook into the "chain" of the previous stitch and draw up a loop, yarn over and draw through one loop on hook (the "chain"), [yarn over and draw through 2 loops on hook] 2 times (the "double crochet"). Repeat step 2 for the length of the foundation.

Join with sc: Place a slip knot on hook, insert hook in indicated stitch, yarn over and draw up a loop, yarn over and draw through both loops on hook.

Pattern Note

Ch-3 at the beginning of each row counts as a dc.

Directions

Body (make 2)

Row 1 (RS): Fdc 103 [115, 127, 139, 151, 163, 175, 187, 199] times. (104 [116, 128, 140, 152, 164, 176, 188, 200] sts)

Row 2: Ch 7 (counts as first dc and ch-4 sp), turn; sk next 4 sts, dc in next 3 sts; *ch 4, sk next 4 sts, dc in next st, ch 4, sk next 4 sts, dc in next 3 sts; rep from * across. (36 [40, 44, 48, 52, 56, 60, 64, 68] dc)

Row 3: Ch 3, turn; dc in next dc, ch 4; *dc in next ch-4 sp, dc in next dc, dc in next ch-4 sp, ch 4, sk next dc, dc in next dc, ch 4; rep from * across to last ch-4 sp; dc in last ch of ch-4 sp, dc in last dc.

Row 4: Ch 13 (counts as first dc and ch-10 sp), turn; skip next 2 dc, dc in next 3 dc; *ch 9, sk next dc, dc in next 3 dc; rep from *across to last 2 dc; ch 5, sk next dc, dc in last dc.

Row 5: Ch 3, turn; dc in first ch-5 sp, ch 4, dc in next 3 dc; *ch 4, dc in 5th ch of next ch-9 sp, ch 4, dc in next 3 dc; rep from * across to last ch-10 sp; ch 4, dc in 5th ch of next ch-10 sp, ch 4, dc in last ch of ch-10 sp, dc in last dc.

Row 6: Ch 7 (counts as first dc and ch-4 sp), turn; *dc in next ch-4 sp, dc in next dc, dc in next ch-4 sp, ch 4, sk next dc, dc in next dc, ch 4; rep from * across to last ch-4 sp; dc in last ch of ch-4 sp, dc in last 2 dc.

Row 7: Ch 3, turn; dc in next 2 dc; *ch 9, sk next dc, dc in next 3 dc; rep from * across to last ch-4 sp; ch 4, dc in last dc.

Row 8: Ch 7 (counts as first dc and ch-4 sp), turn; dc in next 3 dc; *ch 4, dc in 5th ch of next ch-9 sp, ch 4, dc in next 3 dc; rep from * to end.

Row 9: Ch 3, turn; dc in next dc, ch 4; *dc in next ch-4 sp, dc in next dc, dc in next ch-4 sp, ch 4, sk next dc, dc in next dc, ch 4; rep from * across to

last ch-4 sp; dc in last ch of ch-4 sp, dc in last dc.

Rows 10–36 [42, 42, 42, 42, 42, 42, 42, 42]: Repeat Rows 4–9 four [five, five, five, five, five, five, five] times, then rows 4-6 once more.

Left Side

SIZES XS [M, 1X, 2X, 4X] ONLY

Row 37 [–, 43, –, 43, 43, –, 43, –]: Ch 3, turn; dc in next 2 dc; *ch 9, sk next dc, dc in next 3 dc; rep from * 1 [–, 2, –, 3, 3, –, 4, –] times more; ch 4, dc in next dc. (10 [–, 13, –, 16, 16, –, 19, –] dc)

Row 38 [–, 44, –, 44, 44, –, 44, –]: Ch 7 (counts as first dc and ch-4 sp), turn; *dc in next 3 dc, ch 4, dc in 5th ch of next ch-9 sp, ch 4; rep from * to last 3 dc, 3 dc in last 3 dc. (12 [–, 16, –, 20, 20, –, 24, –] dc)

Row 39 [–, 45, –, 45, 45, –, 45, –]: Ch 3, turn; dc in next dc, ch 4; *dc in next ch-4 sp, dc in next dc, dc in next ch-4 sp, ch 4, sk next dc, dc in next dc, ch 4; rep from * across to last ch-4 sp; dc in last ch-4 sp, dc in 3rd ch of ch-7. Fasten off. (12 [–, 16, –, 20, 20, –, 24, –] dc)

SIZES S [L, 3X, 5X] ONLY

Row 43: Ch 3, turn; dc in next 2 dc; *ch 9, sk next dc, dc in next 3 dc; rep from * – [1, –, 2, –, –, 3, –, 4] times more; ch 9, dc in next dc. (– [10, –, 13, –, –, 16, –, 19] dc)

Row 44: Ch 7 (counts as first dc and ch-4 sp), turn; dc in 5th ch of first ch-9 sp; *ch 4, dc in next 3 dc, ch 4, dc in 5th ch of next ch-9 sp; rep from * to last 3 dc, ch 4, 3 dc in last 3 dc. (– [13, –, 17, –, –, 21, –, 25] dc)

Row 45: Ch 3, turn; dc in next dc, ch 4; *dc in next ch-4 sp, dc in next dc, dc in next ch-4 sp, ch 4, sk next dc, dc in next dc, ch 4; rep from * to last two ch-4 sps, dc in next ch-4 sp, dc in next dc, dc in next ch-4 sp, ch 3, dc in 3rd ch of beg ch-7. Fasten off. (– [14, –, 18, –, –, 22, –, 26] dc)

Right Side

SIZES XS [M, 1X, 2X, 4X] ONLY

Row 37 [–, 43, –, 43, 43, –, 43, –]: With right side facing, skip 40 (–, 40, –, 40, 52, –, 52, –) sts (counting chs and dc) from last st of first row of Left Side and join with a sl st in next dc; ch 3, dc in next 2 dc; *ch 9, sk next dc, dc in next 3 dc; rep from * 1 [–, 2, –, 3, 3, –, 4, –] times more; ch 4, dc in next dc. (10 [–, 13, –, 16, 16, –, 19, –] dc)

Row 38 [–, 44, –, 44, 44, –, 44, –]: Ch 7 (counts as first dc and ch-4 sp), turn; dc in next 3 dc; *ch 4, dc in 5th ch of next ch-9 sp, ch 4, dc in next 3 dc; rep from * to end. (12 [–, 16, –, 20, 20, –, 24, –] dc)

Row 39 [–, 45, –, 45, 45, –, 45, –]: Ch 3, turn; dc in next dc, ch 4, sk next dc; *dc in next ch-4 sp, dc in next dc, dc in next ch-4 sp, ch 4, sk next dc, dc in next dc, ch 4; rep from * to last ch-4 sp, dc in last ch of ch-4 sp, dc in last dc. Fasten off. (12 [−, 16, −, 20, 20, −, 24, −] dc)

SIZES S [L, 3X, 5X] ONLY

Row 43: With right side facing, skip − (42, −, 42, −, −, 54, −, 54) sts from last st of first row of Left Side and join with a sl st in next dc; ch 7 (counts as first dc and ch-4 sp), dc in next three dc, *ch 9, sk next dc, dc in next 3 dc; rep from * − [one, −, two, −, −, four, −, five] times more; ch 4, dc in 3rd ch of ch-7. (− [11, −, 14, −, −, 17, −, 20] dc)

Row 44: Ch 7, turn; dc in next 3 dc; *ch 4, dc in 5th ch of next ch-9 sp, ch 4, dc in next 3 dc; rep from * − [one, −, two, −, −, four, −, five] times more; ch 4, dc in 3rd ch of ch-7. (− [13, −, 17, −, −, 21, −, 25] dc)

Row 45: Ch 3, turn; dc in first ch-4 sp, ch 4, sk next dc, dc in next dc, ch 4; *dc in next ch-4 sp, dc in next dc, dc in next ch-4 sp, ch 4, sk next dc, dc in next dc, ch 4; rep from * to last ch-4 sp, dc in last ch of ch-4 sp, dc in 3rd ch of ch-7. (− [13, −, 17, −, −, 21, −, 25] dc)

ALL SIZES

Hem Ribbing

Ch 21.

Row 1: Sc in 2nd ch from hook and in each ch across; with right side facing, sl st in the

bottom of the first Fdc, sl st in next Fdc. (20 sc, 2 sl sts)

Row 2: Turn; sk 2 sl sts, working in BLO, sc in each sc across. (20 sc)

Row 3: Ch 1, turn; working in BLO, sc in each sc across, sl st in next 2 Fdc. (20 sc, 2 sl sts)

Rows 4–104 [116, 128, 140, 152, 164, 176, 188, 200]: Repeat Rows 2 & 3 until all Fdc have been worked, ending with Row 2. Fasten off.

Sleeves (make 2)

Row 1: Fdc 79 [79, 91, 91, 103, 103, 115, 115, 127] times (80 [80, 92, 92, 104, 104, 116, 116, 128] Fdc)

Row 2: Ch 7 (counts as first dc and ch-4 sp), turn; sk next 4 sts, dc in next 3 sts; *ch 4, sk next 4 sts, dc in next st, ch 4, sk next 4 sts, dc in next 3 sts; rep from * across. (28 [28, 32, 32, 36, 36, 40, 40, 44] dc)

Row 3: Ch 3, turn; dc in next dc, ch 4; *dc in next ch-4 sp, dc in next dc, dc in next ch-4 sp, ch 4, sk next dc, dc in next dc, ch 4; rep from * across to last ch-4 sp; sk next 3 ch, dc in next ch, dc in last dc.

Row 4: Ch 13 (counts as first dc and ch-10 space), turn; sk next dc, dc in next 3 dc; *ch 9, sk next dc, dc in next 3 dc; rep from * across to last 2 dc; ch 5, sk next dc, dc in last dc.

Row 5: Ch 3, turn; dc in first ch-5 sp, ch 4, dc in next 3 dc; *ch 4, dc in 5th ch of next ch-9 sp, ch 4, dc in next 3 dc; rep from * across to last ch-10 sp; ch 4, dc in 5th ch of next ch-10 sp, ch 4, dc in last ch of ch-10 sp, dc in last dc.

Row 6: Ch 7 (counts as first dc and ch-4 sp), turn; *dc in next ch-4 sp, dc in next dc, dc in next ch-4 sp, ch 4, sk next dc, dc in next dc, ch 4; rep from * across to last ch-4 sp; dc in last ch of ch-4 sp, dc in last 2 dc.

Row 7: Ch 3, turn; dc in next 2 dc; *ch 9, sk next dc, dc in next 3 dc; rep from * across to last ch-4 sp; ch 4, dc in last dc.

Row 8: Ch 7 (counts as first dc and ch-4 sp), turn; dc in next 3 dc; *ch 4, dc in 5th ch of next ch-9 sp, ch 4, dc in next 3 dc; rep from * to end.

Row 9: Ch 3, turn; dc in next dc, ch 4; *dc in next ch-4 sp, dc in next dc, dc in next ch-4 sp, ch 4, sk next dc, dc in next dc, ch 4; rep from * across to last ch-4 sp; dc in last ch of ch-4 sp, dc in last dc.

Rows 10–21 [21, 21, 21, 21, 21, 21, 27, 27]: Repeat Rows 4–9 two [two, two, two, two, two, two, three, three] times more. Fasten off.

Hem Ribbing

Ch 13.

Row 1: Sc in 2nd ch from hook and in each ch across; with right side facing, sl st in the bottom of the first Fdc, sl st in next Fdc. (12 sc, 2 sl sts)

Row 2: Turn; sk 2 sl sts, working in BLO, sc in each sc across. (12 sc)

Row 3: Ch 1, turn; working in BLO, sc in each sc across, sl st in next 2 Fdc. (12 sc, 2 sl sts)

Rows 4–80 [80, 92, 92, 104, 104, 116, 116, 128]: Repeat Rows 2 & 3 until all Fdc have been worked, ending with Row 2. Fasten off.

Finishing

Weave in all ends. Block all pieces to size given on the schematic.

Using the mattress stitch throughout, sew shoulder seams. Then place two markers on each side edge of front and back about 6.5 [6.5, 7.5, 7.5, 8.5, 8.5, 9.5, 9.5, 10.5]" down from shoulder seam. Sew sleeves between markers. Sew side and sleeve seams.

Mock Turtleneck Finishing

Rnd 1: Join with sc in center back of neck. Evenly space enough single crochets around to end with an even number and to make a smooth finish on the neckline. Too many will cause rippling and too few will tighten the neck too much. Join with a sl st in first sc.

Row 2: Ch 13, sc in 2nd ch from hook and in each ch across; sl st in next sc on neckline. (12 sc, 1 sl st)

Row 2: Turn; sk sl st, working in BLO, sc in each sc across. (12 sc)

Row 3: Ch 1, turn; working in BLO, sc in each sc across, sl st in next 2 sc on neckline. (12 sc, 2 sl sts)

Row 4: Turn; sk 2 sl sts, working in BLO, sc in each sc across. (12 sc)

Repeat Rows 3 & 4 until all neckline sc have been worked, ending with Row 4. Fasten off. Use tail to seam up the turtleneck.

Lightly steam seams and neckline for a professional finish.

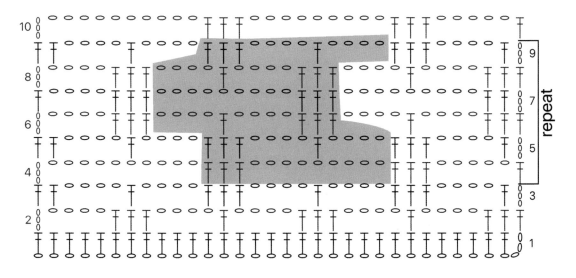

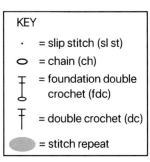

KEY
· = slip stitch (sl st)
◯ = chain (ch)
⊤ = foundation double
   crochet (fdc)
† = double crochet (dc)
⬭ = stitch repeat

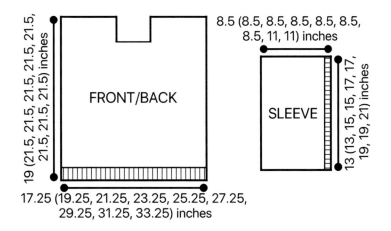

8.5 (8.5, 8.5, 8.5, 8.5, 8.5, 8.5, 11, 11) inches

19 (21.5, 21.5, 21.5, 21.5, 21.5, 21.5, 21.5, 21.5) inches

FRONT/BACK

SLEEVE

13 (13, 15, 15, 17, 17, 19, 19, 21) inches

17.25 (19.25, 21.25, 23.25, 25.25, 27.25, 29.25, 31.25, 33.25) inches

LEFT SIDE, Sizes XS, M, 1X, 2X & 4X Only

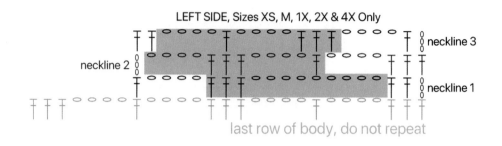

neckline 2

neckline 3

neckline 1

last row of body, do not repeat

LEFT SIDE, Sizes S, L, 3X & 5X Only

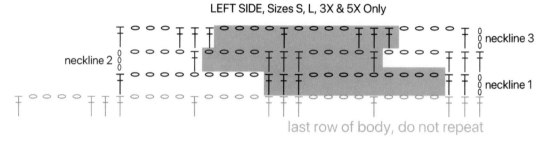

neckline 2

neckline 3

neckline 1

last row of body, do not repeat

RIGHT SIDE, Sizes XS, M, 1X, 2X & 4X Only

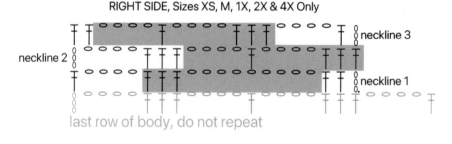

neckline 2

neckline 3

neckline 1

last row of body, do not repeat

RIGHT SIDE, Sizes S, L, 3X & 5X Only

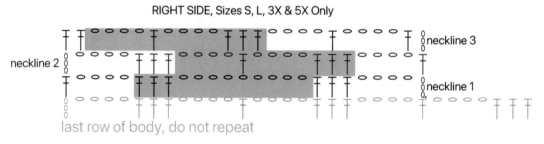

neckline 2

neckline 3

neckline 1

last row of body, do not repeat

Le Semplicità

TRANSLATION: SIMPLICITY

Le Semplicita is truely a simple classic cardigan with just a hint of lace at the bottom. A classic Italian staple stitch of chains, single and double crochet give this drop-sleeve cardigan a bit of class.

Finished Sizes

XS [S, M, L, 1X, 2X, 3X, 4X, 5X]

Finished Bust

31 [41, 43.5, 48.5, 53, 55.5, 60.5, 63, 68] inches
78.5 [104, 110.5, 123, 134.5, 141, 153.5, 160, 172.5] cm

Finished Length

22.5 [23, 23.25, 23.5, 23.75, 24, 24, 24.5, 24.5] inches
57 [58.5, 59, 59.5, 60.5, 61, 61, 62, 62] cm

Materials

1470 [1850, 1940, 2100, 2280, 2430, 2510, 2640, 2770] yards (1345 [1690, 1775, 1920, 2085, 2220, 2295, 2415, 2535] m) lace-weight yarn

Sample uses Black Trillium Fibres Silken Lace (85% Superwash Merino / 15% Mulberry Silk; 7.05 oz / 200 g = 1450 yards / 1326 m) in the color Raspberry

Crochet Hook

Size 3.00 mm or size needed for gauge.

Notions

10 [10, 10, 10, 10, 10, 10, 11, 11] 1-inch (2.5 cm) buttons

4 stitch markers

Gauge

24 dc and 14 dc rows = 4 inches (10 cm)

Special Stitches

Fdc: Foundation double crochet (This technique creates a foundation chain and a row of double crochet stitches in one)

Step 1: Place a slip knot on hook, ch 4, yarn over, insert hook in 4th ch from hook and draw up a loop; yarn over and draw through one loop on hook (the "chain"); [yarn over and draw through 2 loops on hook] 2 times (the "double crochet").

Step 2: Yarn over, insert hook into the "chain" of the previous stitch and draw up a loop, yarn over and draw through one loop on hook (the "chain"), [yarn over and draw through 2 loops on hook] 2 times (the "double crochet"). Repeat step 2 for the length of the foundation.

Pattern Notes

Ch-3 at the beginning of designated rows counts as the first dc of that row.

Ch-1 at the beginning of designated rows does not count as a stitch.

Directions

Back

Row 1 (RS): Fdc 100 [132, 140, 156, 172, 180, 196, 204, 220] times. (101 [133, 141, 157, 173, 181, 197, 205, 221] total fdc)

Row 2: Ch 3, turn; dc in next 2 dc; *ch 3, sk 2 fdc, sc in next 3 fdc, ch 3, sk 2 fdc, dc in next fdc; rep from * across to last 2 fdc; dc in last 2 fdc. (17 [21, 22, 24, 26, 27, 29, 30, 32] dc, 12 [16, 17, 19, 21, 22, 24, 25, 27] 3-sc groups)

Row 3: Ch 1, turn; sc in first 3 dc; *sc in next ch-3 sp, ch 3, sk next sc, dc in next sc, ch 3, sc in next ch-3 sp, sc in next dc; rep from * across to last 2 dc; sc in last 2 dc.

Row 4: Ch 3, turn; dc in next 2 sc, *ch 3, sc in next ch-3 sp, sc in next dc, sc in next ch-3 sp, ch 3, sk next sc, dc in next sc; rep from * across to last 2 sc, dc in last 2 sc.

Row 5: Rep Row 3.

Rows 6–23: Rep Rows 4 & 5 eighteen times.

Row 24: Ch 3, turn; evenly space 100 [132, 140, 156, 172, 180, 196, 204, 220] dc across by working 2 dc in each ch-3 sp and 1 dc in each st. (101 [133, 141, 157, 173, 181, 197, 205, 221] dc)

Row 25: Ch 3, turn; dc in next dc and in each dc across.

Rows 2– 78 [80, 82, 82, 84, 84, 84, 86, 86]: Rep Row 25.

Right Back

Row 79 [81, 83, 83, 85, 85, 85, 87, 87]: Ch 3, turn; dc in next 27 [43, 44, 52, 60, 63, 70, 74, 80] dc, leaving rem sts unworked. (28 [44, 45, 53, 61, 64, 71, 75, 81] dc)

Row 80 [82, 84, 84, 86, 86, 86, 88, 88]: Ch 3, turn; dc in next dc and in each dc across.

Row 81 [83, 85, 85, 87, 87, 87, 89, 89]: Ch 3, turn; dc in next dc and in each dc across.

Fasten off.

Left Back

Row 79 [81, 83, 83, 85, 85, 85, 87, 87]: Sk next 45 [45, 51, 51, 51, 53, 55, 55, 59] dc after last

dc of first Right Back row; join with a sl st in next dc, ch 3; dc to end. (28 [44, 45, 53, 61, 64, 71, 75, 81] dc)

Row 80 [82, 84, 84, 86, 86, 86, 88, 88]: Ch 3, turn; dc in next dc and in each dc across.

Row 81 [83, 85, 85, 87, 87, 87, 89, 89]: Ch 3, turn; dc in next dc and in each dc across. Fasten off.

Left Front

Row 1 (RS): Fdc 52 [68, 68, 76, 84, 92, 100, 100, 108] times. (53 [69, 69, 77, 85, 93, 101, 101, 109] total fdc)

Row 2: Ch 3 turn; dc in next 2 dc; *ch 3, sk 2 fdc, sc in next 3 fdc, ch 3, sk 2 fdc, dc in next fdc; rep from * across to last 2 fdc; dc in last 2 fdc. (11 [13, 13, 14, 15, 16, 17, 17, 18] dc, 6 [8, 8, 9, 10, 11, 12, 12, 13] 3-sc groups)

Row 3: Ch 1, turn; sc in first 3 dc; *sc in next ch-3 sp, ch 3, sk next sc, dc in next sc, ch 3, sc in next ch-3 sp, sc in next dc; rep from * across to last 2 dc; sc in last 2 dc.

Row 4: Ch 3, turn; dc in next 2 dc, *ch 3, sc in next ch-3 sp, sc in next dc, sc in next ch-3 sp, ch 3, sk next sc, dc in next sc; rep from * across to last 2 sc, dc in last 2 sc.

Row 5: Rep Row 3.

Rows 6–23: Rep Rows 4 & 5 eighteen times.

Row 24: Ch 3, turn; evenly space 52 [68, 68, 76, 84, 92, 100, 100, 108] dc across by working 2 dc in each ch-3 sp and 1 dc in each st. (53 [69, 69, 77, 85, 93, 101, 101, 109] total dc)

Row 25: Ch 3, turn; dc in next dc and in each dc across.

Rows 26–75 [77, 79, 79, 81, 81, 81, 83, 83]: Rep Row 25.

Row 76 [78, 80, 80, 82, 82, 82, 84, 84]: Ch 3, turn; dc in next 27 [43, 44, 52, 60, 63, 70, 74, 80] dc, leaving rem sts unworked. (28 [44, 45, 53, 61, 64, 71, 75, 81] dc)

Row 77 [79, 81, 81, 83, 83, 83, 85, 85]: Ch 3, turn; dc in next dc and in each dc across.

Rows 78 [80, 82, 82, 84, 84, 84, 86, 86] – 81 [83, 85, 85, 87, 87, 87, 89, 89]: Ch 3, turn; dc in next dc and in each dc across. Fasten off.

Right Front

Rows 1–75 [77, 79, 79, 81, 81, 81, 83, 83]: Rep Rows 1–75 [77, 79, 79, 81, 81, 81, 83, 83] of Left Front.

Row 76 [78, 80, 80, 82, 82, 82, 84, 84]: Turn; sl st in first 26 [26, 25, 25, 25, 30, 31, 27, 29], ch 3 (counts as first dc); dc in next dc and in each dc to end. (28 [44, 45, 53, 61, 64, 71, 75, 81] dc)

Row 77 [79, 81, 81, 83, 83, 83, 85, 85]: Ch 3, turn; dc in next dc and in each dc across.

Rows 78 [80, 82, 82, 84, 84, 84, 86, 86] – 81 [83, 85, 85, 87, 87, 87, 89, 89]: Ch 3, turn; dc in next dc and in each dc across. Fasten off.

Sleeves (make 2)

Row 1: Fdc 51 [65, 65, 65, 65, 65, 65, 77, 77] times. (52 [66, 66, 66, 66, 66, 66, 78, 78] fdc)

Row 2: Ch 3, turn; dc in next fdc and each fdc across.

Row 3: Ch 3, turn; 2 dc in next dc, dc in each dc to last 2 dc, 2 dc in next dc, dc in last dc. (54 [68, 68, 68, 68, 68, 68, 80, 80] dc)

Row 4: Ch 3, turn; dc in next dc and each dc across.

Rows 5–44 [36, 44, 36, 28, 20, 28, 36, 26]: Rep rows 3 & 4 another 20 [16, 20, 16, 12, 8, 12, 16, 11] times. (94 [98, 108, 100, 92, 84, 92, 112, 102] dc

SIZES XS [S, L, IX, 2X, 3X, 5X] ONLY

Rows 45–46 [37–39, –, 37–43, 29–40, 21–40, 29–36, –, 27–32]: Rep Row 3 another 2 [3, –, 7, 12, 20, 8, –, 6] times. (98 [104, –, 114, 116, 124, 108, –, 114] dc at the end of the last row)

ALL SIZES

Rows 47–48 [40–46, 45–46, 44–45, 41–42, 41–42, 37–38, 37–38, 33–34]: Rep Row 4. Fasten off. (98 [104, 108, 114, 116, 124, 108, 112, 114] dc

Finishing

Weave in all ends. Block all pieces to size given on the schematic.

Using the mattress stitch throughout, sew shoulder seams. Then place two markers on each side edge of front and back about 7.5 [8, 8.5, 9, 9, 9.5, 8.5, 8.5, 9]" down from shoulder seam. Sew sleeves between markers. Beginning at hem edge, sew side and sleeve seams.

Neck Finishing

Row 1: With right side facing, join with sl st to st at neckline edge of Right Front, sc evenly across Right Front, Back, and Left Front, placing last st in st at neckline edge of Left Front. The number of stitches doesn't matter as long as the neckline doesn't buckle or pucker.

Rows 2–9: Ch 1, turn; sc in each sc across. At the end of Row 9, fasten off.

Button Band

Row 1: With right side facing and working along the row edges of the Left Front, evenly space 145 [146, 150, 150, 154, 154, 154, 159, 159] sc across to top of neckline sts.

Rows 2–9: Ch 1, turn; sc in each sc across. At the end of Row 9, fasten off.

Buttonhole Band

Row 1: With right side facing and working along the row edges of the Right Front, evenly space 145 [146, 150, 150, 154, 154, 154, 159, 159] sc across to top of neckline sts.

Rows 2–4: Ch 1, turn; sc in each sc across.

Row 5: Ch 1, turn; sc in first 3 [3, 5, 5, 7, 7, 7, 2, 2] sc, ch 4, sk 4 sc; *sc in next 11 sc, ch 4, sk next 4 sc; rep from * 8 [8, 8, 8, 8, 8, 8, 9, 9] more times; sc in last 3 [4, 6, 6, 8, 8, 8, 3, 3] sc.

Row 6: Ch 1, turn; *sc in each st to next ch-4 sp, 4 sc in ch-4 sp; rep from * to last 3 [4, 6, 6, 8, 8, 8, 3, 3] sts; sc to end.

Rows 7–9: Rep rows 2–4. At the end of Row 9, fasten off.

Weave in all remaining ends. Sew buttons on button band to correspond with the buttonholes. Lightly steam to shape.

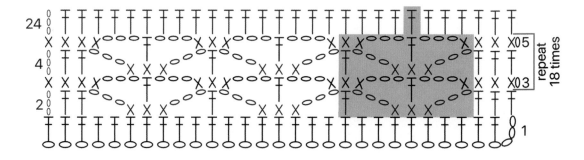

24

4

2

1

repeat
18 times

X05

X03

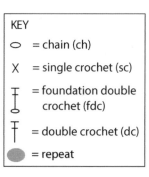

KEY

○ = chain (ch)

X = single crochet (sc)

⊥ = foundation double
crochet (fdc)

† = double crochet (dc)

⬭ = repeat

15.5 [20.5, 21.5, 24, 26.5, 28, 30.5, 31.5, 34]"

(back width)

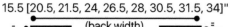

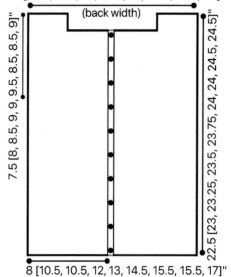

7.5 [8, 8.5, 9, 9, 9.5, 8.5, 8.5, 9]"

22.5 [23, 23.25, 23.5, 23.75, 24, 24, 24.5, 24.5]"

8 [10.5, 10.5, 12, 13, 14.5, 15.5, 15.5, 17]"

15 [16, 16.75, 17.5, 18, 19,
16.75, 17.25, 17.5]"

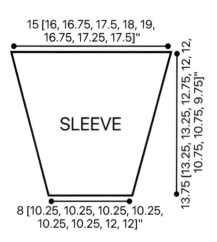

SLEEVE

13.75 [13.25, 13.25, 12.75, 12, 12,
10.75, 10.75, 9.75]"

8 [10.25, 10.25, 10.25, 10.25,
10.25, 10.25, 12, 12]"

Uncinetto Legato

TRANSLATION: CROCHET LEGACY

If you have followed me from the beginning, the original name of my business was Crochet Legacy, dedicated to my Nonna. Uncinetto Legato is a nod to where I started. Lavish lace on the edge is tempered by a simple body of texture. It looks so complicated but only you will know how quick it was to make.

Finished Size

55 inches (140 cm) wide on top edge by 32 inches (81 cm) deep (blocked)

Materials

925 yards (846 m) laceweight yarn

Sample is made with Stunning String Studio Lavish Lace (100% superwash merino; 3.5 oz / 100g = 925 yards / 846 m) in the color Deep Water

Crochet Hook

Size 3.0 mm or size needed for gauge

Notions

Stitch marker
Yarn needle

Gauge

24 dc and 11 dc rows = 4 inches (10 cm), blocked

Special Stitches

Bobble: [Yarn over twice, insert hook in indicated stitch, yarn over and draw up a loop (4 loops remain on hook); (yarn over and draw through two loops on hook) twice] four times in same stitch (5 loops remain on hook); yarn over and draw through all 5 loops on hook.

Pattern Notes

Do not skip the first dc when starting a new row unless otherwise indicated.

The ch-4 at the beginning of each row counts as the first dc and ch-1 space.

Directions

Ch 5.

Row 1: Dc in 5th ch from hook (skipped chs count as first dc and ch-1 sp), [ch 1, dc in same ch] 3 times; PM in middle dc for stitch placement and move up each row to middle dc. (5 dc, 4 ch-1 sps)

Row 2: Ch 4, turn; dc in first dc, dc in each ch-1 sp and dc to marked st; (dc, ch 1, dc, ch 1, dc) in marked st; dc in each ch-1 sp and dc to turning ch-sp; dc in turning-ch sp, (dc, ch 1, dc) in 3rd ch of ch-4 turning ch. (13 dc, 4 ch-1 sps)

Row 3: Ch 4, turn; dc in first dc, dc in first ch-1 sp, dc in each dc to next ch-1 sp; dc in next ch-1 sp, (dc, ch 1, dc, ch 1, dc) in marked st; dc in next ch-1 sp, dc in each dc to turning-ch sp; dc in turning ch-sp, (dc, ch 1, dc) in 3rd ch of ch-4 turning ch. (21 dc, 4 ch-1 sps)

Rows 4–20: Rep row 3. (At end of row 20: 157 dc, 4 ch-1 sps)

Row 21: Ch 4, turn; dc in first dc, dc in first ch-1 sp, ch 1, sk next dc, *dc in next dc, ch 1, sk next dc; rep from * across to ch-1 sp before marked st; dc in ch-1 sp, (dc, ch 1, dc, ch 1, dc) in marked st; dc in next ch-1 sp, ch 1, sk next dc, **dc in next dc, ch 1, sk next dc; rep from ** to turning ch-sp; dc in turning-ch sp, (dc, ch 1, dc) in

3rd ch of ch-4 turning ch. (87 dc, 82 ch-1 sps)

Row 22: Ch 4, turn; dc in first dc, dc in each ch-1 sp and dc to marked stitch; (dc, ch 1, dc, ch 1, dc) in marked stitch; dc in each ch-1 sp and dc across to turning ch-sp; dc in turning-ch sp, (dc, ch 1, dc) in 3rd ch of ch-4 turning ch. (173 dc, 4 ch-1 sps)

Rows 23–24: Rep row 3. (At end of row 24: 189 dc, 4 ch-1 sps)

Rows 25–36: Rep rows 21–24 three times. (At end of row 36: 285 dc, 4 ch-1 sps)

Row 37: Rep row 21. (151 dc, 146 ch-1 sps)

Row 38: Rep row 22. (301 dc, 4 ch-1 sps)

Row 39: Rep row 3. (309 dc, 4 ch-1 sps)

Rows 40–45: Rep rows 37–39 twice. (At end of row 45: 357 dc, 4 ch-1 sps)

Rows 46–53: Rep rows 21–22 four times. (At end of row 53: 421 dc, 4 ch-1 sps)

Edging

Row 54: Ch 9, turn; sk first 7 dc, sc in next dc, *ch 8, sk 6 dc, sc in next dc; rep from * to last 6 dc before marked st; ch 8, sc in next ch-1 sp; ch 3, sk marked st, move marker to ch-3 sp, sc in next ch-1 sp, **ch 8, sk 6 dc, sc in next dc; rep from ** to end, placing last sc in 3rd ch of

ch-4 turning ch. (62 sc, 59 ch-8 sps, 1 ch-9 sp, 1 ch-3 sp)

Row 55: Ch 8 (counts as first tr and ch-4 sp), turn; sc in first ch-8 sp; [ch 8, sc in next ch-8 sp] 29 times; ch 3, sc in marked ch-3 sp, ch 3, sc in next ch-8 sp; [ch 8, sc in next ch-8 sp] 28 times; ch 8, sc in ch-9 sp, ch 4, tr in first ch of ch-9. (58 ch-8 sps, 2 ch-3 sps, 2 ch-4 sps, 2 tr)

Row 56: Ch 7 (counts as first tr and ch-3 sp), turn; [bobble,

ch 3] 3 times in first ch-8 sp, *sc in next ch-8 sp, ch 3, [bobble, ch 3] 3 times in next ch-8 sp; rep from * across to ch-3 sp; sc in ch-3 sp, ch 3, move marker to ch-3 sp just made, sc in next ch-3 sp, ch 3, [bobble, ch 3] 3 times in next ch-8 sp, **sc in next ch-8 sp, ch 3, [bobble, ch 3] 3 times in next ch-8 sp; rep from ** to last sc; tr in 4th ch of ch-8 turning ch. (90 bobbles)

Row 57: Ch 7 (counts as first tr and ch-3 sp), turn; *[bobble in next ch-3 sp, ch 3] 4 times, tr in next sc, ch 3; rep from * to last 3 bobbles before marked ch-3 sp; [bobble in next ch-3 sp, ch 3] 4 times, tr in marked ch-3 sp, ch 3; [bobble in next ch-3 sp, ch 3] 4 times, **tr in next sc, ch 3, [bobble in next ch-3 sp, ch 3] 4 times; rep from ** to end, tr in 4th ch of ch-7 turning ch. (120 bobbles)

Row 58: Ch 1, turn; sc in first tr, ch 1, sc in first ch-3 sp, ch 3, sc in next ch-3 sp, ch 3, 4 dc in next ch-3 sp, *[ch 3, sc in next ch-3 sp] 4 times, ch 3, 4 dc in next ch-3 sp; rep from * to last 2 bobbles before marked tr; ch 3, [sc in next ch-3 sp, ch 3]

twice, dc in marked tr, [ch 3, sc in next ch-3 sp] twice, ch 3, 4 dc in next ch-3 sp, *[ch 3, sc in next ch-3 sp] 4 times, ch 3, 4 dc in next ch-3 sp; rep from ** to last 2 bobbles; [ch 3, sc in next ch-3 sp] twice, ch 1, sc in 4th ch of ch-7 turning ch. (30 4-dc groups)

Row 59: Ch 1, turn; sc in first sc, ch 3, [sc in next ch-3 sp, ch 3] twice, sk next dc, dc in next 2 dc; *ch 3, [sc in next ch-3 sp, ch 3] 5 times, sk next dc, dc in next 2 dc; rep from * to last 3 ch sps before marked dc; [ch 3, sc in next ch-3 sp] 6 times, ch 3, move marker to last ch-3 sp (offset from center), **sk next dc, dc in next 2 dc, ch 3, [sc in next ch-3 sp, ch 3] 5 times; rep

from ** to last 4-dc group, sk next dc, dc in next 2 dc, [ch 3, sc in next ch-3 sp] twice, ch 3, sc in last sc. (181 ch-3 sps)

Row 60: Ch 1, turn; sc in first sc, [3 sc in next ch-3 sp] 3 times, sc in next dc, ch 3, sc in next dc, *[3 sc in next ch-3 sp] 6 times, sc in next dc, ch 3, sc in next dc; rep from * to marked ch-3 sp; [3 sc in next ch-3 sp] 7 times, sc in next dc, ch 3, sc in next dc, **[3 sc in next ch-3 sp] 6 times, sc in next dc, ch 3, sc in next dc; rep from ** to last 3 ch-3 sps; [3 sc next ch-3 sp] 3 times, sc in last sc. (605 sc)

Fasten off.

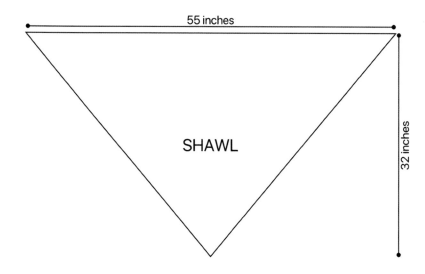

55 inches

SHAWL

32 inches

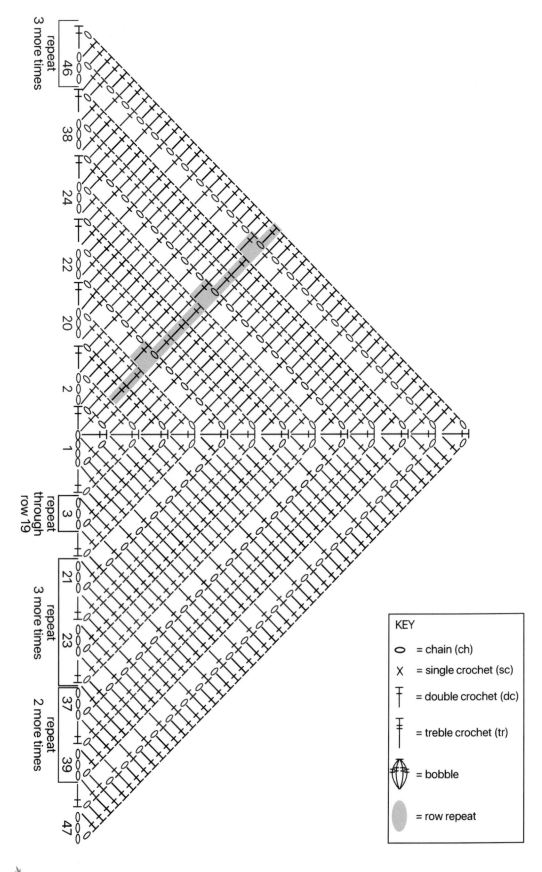

KEY

O = chain (ch)

X = single crochet (sc)

T = double crochet (dc)

‡ = treble crochet (tr)

= bobble

= row repeat

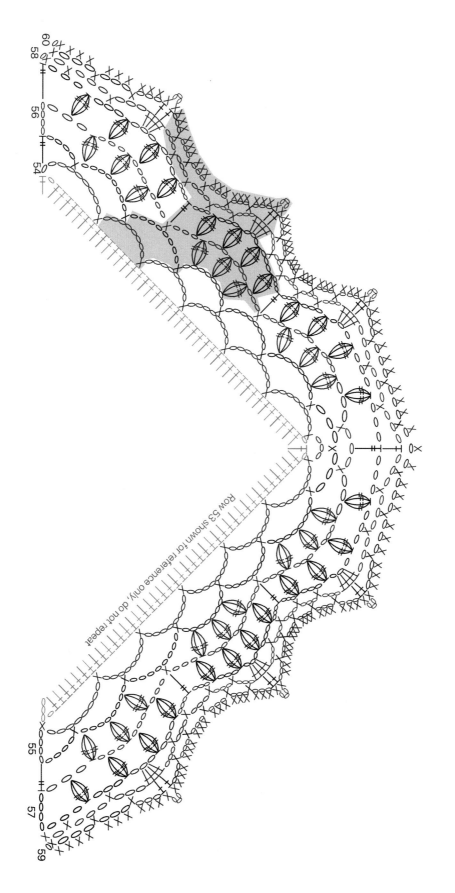

Row 53 shown for reference only, do not repeat

Acknowledgments

I know I say this every time, but each time I set out to write a new book, I find the following statement to be true. Writing a book is tough, coming up with a plan for future books is even tougher. But I have had a team whose love and enthusiasm for me and my ~~crazy~~ *ahem* wonderful ideas have propelled me through.

First and foremost, I must thank God my Almighty Father for giving me this talent of crochet and design and for showing me that I could cultivate it and use it to better myself and to enrich the lives of others. "As each one has received a special gift, employ it in serving one another, as good stewards of the manifold grace of God." – I Peter 4:10

My husband David has been with me on this adventure from the get-go. Thank you for being my rock, listening to me when I planned, dreamed, cried, and didn't want to go on. But most of all, thank you for being you and loving me through all the crazy.

Tyler and Cassie, thank you for being my biggest cheerleaders! You have worn the oversized sweaters I have made you when you were kids, have been my models for patterns over the years (sometimes grudgingly but still with smiles) and I can always count on you to tell everyone you know about your mom the "knitwear designer". I love you both to the moon and back.

On the technical side of things, thank you to the tech editor and graphic artist behind all my stitch charts and schematics - Amy Curtin. Thank you for putting up with me and my delays! Thanks to you I have beautifully clear and mesmerizing charts, clear and understandable patterns and you make sure that every pattern is consistent! (And the math is good!) You are amazing!

Thank you to Gale Zucker for the absolutely incredible photography. I wish I could have taken us to a beautiful Tuscan Winery for the shoot, but you found a wonderful location that fit the theme! You also made my pieces sparkle and shine. I cannot thank you enough!

Thank you to my fabulous graphic artist, Elizabeth Green for the beautiful artistry of the book's layout. You and have helped me craft the image in my head into the stunning pages we see right here. My gratitude is endless!

Thank you to the absolutely stunning model, Yasmin Hasan. You made every one of my designs come alive with the beauty and elegance that I wanted!

Thank you to my pattern testers; Debbie Paul, Katie Lewellen, Marina Koper, Sheree Neumann, Alana Dutton, Juanita Quinones, and Renee Zinck. Thank you for raising questions that both my tech editor and I didn't catch the first time through. You are the best!

And finally, thank you to all of my crochet tribe. It is because of each of you I can continue to share my passion. You are my inspiration and my fiber family.

Resources

Yarns

Feel free to substitute yarns. If you do substitute, you must realize that you will have to verify your gauge, and if you change the weight of yarn, you will almost definitely need a different amount of yarn than listed in the pattern.

Architeturra uses Polka Dot Sheep Tenderfoot (80% merino / 20% nylon; 400 yards/366m = 3.5 oz/100g) in colors (A) Pygmy Owl and (B) Pumpkin. polkadotsheep.com

Costiera uses Wooly Wonka Arianrhod Sock (75% Merino / 20% silk / 5% glitter; 3.5 oz/100g = 435 yds/398 m) in the color Sea Dragon. woolywonkafiber.com

Piazza uses Wooly Wonka Fibers Nimue Sock (50% silk / 50% superwash merino; 3.5 oz / 100g = 435 yds / 398 m) in the colorway Hydrangea. woolywonkafiber.com

Strade uses Anzula Breeze (65% silk / 35% linen; 4.02 oz / 114 g = 750 yards / 685m) in the colorway Birdie. anzula.com

Finestrelle uses Emma's Yarn Super Silky (80% merino / 20% silk; 3.5 oz/100g =

400 yards/366m) in the color Arches. emmasyarn.com

Il Velo da Sposa uses Round Table Yarns Isolde (55% superwash BFL / 45% silk; 3.5 oz / 100g = 875 yards /800m) in the color Uther. roundtableyarns.com

Maniche e Sciarpa uses Schmutzerella Yarns Spectacular (75% Superwash Merino / 20% Nylon / 5% Stellina; 3.5 oz / 100g = 438 yards / 400m) in the color 3 Up, 2 Across. schmutzerellayarns.com

Parentesi uses Emma's Yarn Beautifully Basic (100% Superwash Merino; 3.5 oz / 100 g = 438 yards / 400 m) in the color Wish You Were Beer. emmasyarn.com

Le Semplicità uses Black Trillium Fibres Silken Lace (85% Superwash Merino / 15% Mulberry Silk; 7.05 oz / 200 g = 1450 yards / 1326 m) in the color Raspberry. blacktrilliumfibres.com

Uncinetto Legato uses Stunning String Studio Lavish Lace (100% superwash merino; 3.5 oz / 100g = 925 yards / 846 m) in the color Deep Water. stunningstring.com

Blocking Supplies

KnitIQ No Rinse Delicate Wash knitiq.com/collections/all/ products/no-rinse-delicate-wool-wash-lavender-citrus-fragrance-16-9oz

KnitIQ Blocking Mats knitiq.com/collections/all/ products/extra-thick-block-ing-mats-with-grids-pins-storage-bag

Inspinknity, LLC, Blocking Wires inspinknity.com

Crochet Hooks

Addi® Comfort Grip Hooks www.skacelknitting.com/ Addi-Comfort-Grip-Hook-Color-Coded-Handle

About the Author

Karen Whooley is an award-winning, internationally known crochet designer, author, and instructor. She develops patterns and teaches classes for crocheters who want simplicity and elegance wrapped up in adventure.

Karen is the author of *Pineapple Passion*, *Coastal Crochet*, *A Garden of Shawls*, *Crochet Rocks Socks* and 18 other books as well as many patterns published in books and magazines. Her classes both online and live are some of the most sought after in the crochet genre. Crochet is her passion and she wants to take that passion and inspire crocheters in any way she can. Most importantly, Karen wants to bring each crocheter self-confidence and enable them to take what they have learned from her designs and classes so that they can happily create whatever spurs their own crochet passion.

Find her at KarenWhooley.com

FYI: Karen's newsletter list gets sneak previews, tips, and tricks, deep discounts on new products, and is the first to know about new patterns, books and classes. Sign up at karenwhooley.com/subscribe

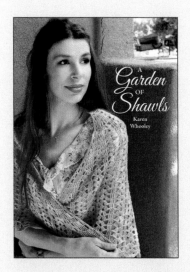

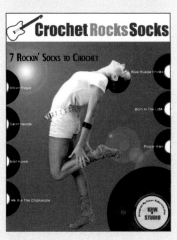

If you enjoyed Modern Italian Lace Crochet

I would appreciate it if you would leave a review on Amazon, Goodreads, and/or BookBub. Even a line or two would be incredibly helpful.

Other Titles by Karen Whooley

A Garden Of Shawls
amzn.to/2Iubvuq

Crochet Rocks Socks
amzn.to/2GusU9H

Coastal Crochet
amzn.to/2PeUB8Y

Pineapple Passion
amzn.to/2RI7Vo5

Notes